F. W. FROHAWK

His Life and Work

F.W. Frohawk (1861–1946)

F. W. FROHAWK

His Life and Work

JUNE CHATFIELD

The Crowood Press

First published in 1987 by
The Crowood Press
Ramsbury, Marlborough
Wiltshire SN8 2HE

© text June Chatfield 1987

© Frohawk illustrations Valezina Bolingbroke, except page 19
Ipswich Museum; pages 27, 30 and 164 National Museum of Wales,
Cardiff; pages 119, 123 and 127 British Museum (Natural History)

British Library Cataloguing in Publication Data

Chatfield, June E.
F.W. Frohawk : his life and work.
1. Frohawk, F.W.   2. Naturalists–Great
Britain–Biography
I. Title
508'.092'4   QH31.F88

ISBN 0–946284–68–7

Typeset by Inforum Ltd, Portsmouth
Printed in Great Britain

Contents

Foreword

In an age when we are almost overwhelmed by lavishly illustrated natural history books, it is hard to visualise the impact F. W. Frohawk's illustrations made fifty or sixty years ago. It is therefore with great pleasure that I welcome Dr June Chatfield's book, which evaluates both Frohawk's artistic and scientific work, and elegantly weaves his work and his association with many eminent Victorian and later naturalists into the story of his life.

Frohawk's illustrations were familiar to me from an early age. I often used the books he illustrated and many of my generation must have been captivated by the freshness and accuracy of his work. He was a rare individual, a keen naturalist who, by his talent as an artist, could share his fascination for animals with a wide audience. I always think first of Frohawk's paintings of butterflies, which must rank with the finest ever produced, but he also painted many other animals, illustrating a wide range of professional monographs on subjects ranging from fishes to birds, all with the careful observation and skilful interpretation that characterise his work.

A visit to the British Museum (Natural History) today will show many budding artists carefully studying the exhibits. Frohawk also used the collections there as a source of information and to check minute details of specimens, and he was commissioned by many scientists at the Museum to illustrate their works. Some of these studies have become classics, and although the text of many have stood the test of time, the main reason that they are now highly prized must be for their illustrations. Frohawk's illustrations were frequently copied and used in subsequent works. In a number of well-known works the comment appears 'I wish to thank . . . for allowing the beautiful originals of F. W. Frohawk's *Natural History of British Butterflies* to be copied', and he is credited with the original observation of the association of ants and blue butterflies, the subsequent evaluation of which has enabled us to understand an unexpected link, important in conservation.

However, it is not only as an illustrator that we remember Frohawk, but also for his extensive field observations which he published and which have been widely used and quoted. It was his natural history observation and field work which enabled him to add more than just artistic ability to his paintings. He made a major contribution to science with his study of the life history of British butterflies, and his classic book on the variation of the colours and patterns of British butterflies. Frohawk's works contain many original observations, often quoted by subsequent authors, and these works are still used now, although some of his books have become collector's items and are out of the range of many aspiring naturalists. Although they may not have realised it, for many years the public bought copies of his water-colours when they were sold as postcards and included in booklets on butterflies produced by the British Museum (Natural History).

Frohawk made careful notes with his drawings, and these are now a valuable part of the Frohawk archives at the British Museum (Natural History). He was an active member of the South London Entomological and Natural History Society, exhibiting specimens and drawings and discussing his science and art with Lord Rothschild, Lord Walsingham and many of the other influential scientists of the day. He was a Fellow of the Entomological Society (now the Royal Entomological Society) and, for his contribution to entomological science, he was made an Honorary Fellow.

Frohawk probably derived much interest from his field work and this is clear in his writings and in the lifelike illustrations he produced. He collected butterflies and moths as a means of studying them, and his main collection went to Lord Rothschild and is now preserved in the British Museum (Natural History), while some specimens he collected are in the National Museum of Wales, Cardiff.

Frohawk was a regular contributor to one of the great country magazines of Britain, *The Field*, which over the years published his drawings, his letters and eventually appointed him natural history editor, a post he held for many years. He was also editor of entomological journals and was the pivot for much of the entomological work of the time.

F. W. Frohawk's work can be ranked with that of the distinguished natural history illustrators, from Bewick to Tunnicliffe. Dr Chatfield's sympathetic study is a fascinating account of the man, his times and his art.

Dr Paul Whalley
Department of Entomology
British Museum (Natural History)

Preface

In 1982, as Curator of The Gilbert White Museum at Selborne, I received a letter from Valezina, Viscountess Bolingbroke asking for advice on the collection of drawings and paintings by her father, the naturalist and illustrator F. W. Frohawk. I accordingly made a visit to Pulborough in West Sussex and returned with a collection of pictures and plans for an exhibition. This went on display in Selborne in 1983, subsequently touring other museums over the next two years.

Frohawk's art is very direct and realistic, and as such appeals to people from all walks of life, but it is particularly appreciated by naturalists for the accurate detail and sympathetic treatment of the subject. It is always particularly exciting to see rough drawings, as these give an insight into the artist at work: the Frohawk collection had many working drawings from very rough pencil sketches, even on the backs of envelopes or postcards, through more detailed drawings to final art work ready for publication.

Valezina, Frohawk's youngest and only surviving daughter, also gave a vivid insight into Frohawk's world, with its roots in Victorian natural history, through her recollections about her father, his work and fellow naturalists.

In his last few years Frohawk wrote an account of his life and many quotations from this highly readable, but as yet unpublished, manuscript are given throughout. These are presented with very little editing apart from corrections of spelling and obvious slips of the pen. After a brief biographical section, the book explores various aspects of Frohawk's life and his development as a naturalist, illustrator and writer.

Although he was a good ornithologist and a fine bird illustrator, Frohawk made his particular mark in entomology as author of a standard two-volume classic the *Natural History of British Butterflies*. This took twenty years to complete and involved much original research, with Frohawk illustrating the full life cycles of all the British species of butterflies as well as writing the text. He also wrote and illustrated *The Complete Book of British Butterflies* and *Varieties of British Butterflies*. In addition to these books, Frohawk contributed many articles to scientific journals and to *The Field* over a period of sixty years.

Various friends and colleagues have helped with this book. I would like to acknowledge first the help of Valezina, Viscountess Bolingbroke who made the collection of her father's work freely available for study and reproduction and whose first-hand account and memory of events were an invaluable resource. She also read and commented on the text.

Preface

Library facilities are essential to a project on such a prolific author and illustrator and I am grateful to the library staff of the British Museum (Natural History) in London, the National Museum of Wales, Cardiff, and the Hampshire County Library Service, Winchester. Mr John Kenyon and Mr Peter Morgan of the National Museum of Wales alerted me to some useful references. Other information was provided by Dr Julian Vincent (University of Reading) Mr Michel Hughes, Dr Gerald Legg (Booth Museum, Brighton) and Mr Alastair Aston. Dr D. H. and Mrs Claire Dalby kindly gave help on the artist's techniques and materials, while most of the photography was undertaken by Mr Erick Broadbent. For reading and commenting on the typescript, thanks are due to Mrs Janet Ridout Sharpe and Mr Matthew Oates. The foreword was written by Dr Paul Whalley, lepidopterist at the British Museum (Natural History), and I am grateful to other members of the Department of Entomology at the Museum for access to Frohawk material in their collections and for their help in entomological matters. The Ipswich Museum kindly gave permission for the reproduction of a pencil drawing by Frohawk from their collections. For an introduction to The Crowood Press, I am indebted to Mr John Clegg. Other assistance was received from Mrs Deidre Clenet, Mr Eric Philip (Maidstone Museum) and Mrs Heather Tait.

June Chatfield
Alton, Hampshire, 1986

Introduction

The naturalist and illustrator, Frederick William Frohawk, was born at Brisley Hall, East Dereham in Norfolk on 16 July 1861. He was the youngest of five children of Francis William Frohawk, a gentleman farmer, and his wife Lydia Drage: there were two girls and three boys, with the eldest boy, Francis, considerably older than the rest. Francis (known as Frank) was in the Royal Navy, where he rapidly rose to the rank of Commander before his premature death in the year of Queen Victoria's Jubilee (1887). However, because of the difference in ages (Frank was about fourteen years Frohawk's senior), and with Frank being away so much at sea, his life did not appear to overlap very much with that of his young brother Frederick. The two younger brothers, William and Frederick, were more of an age, and sometimes shared childhood expeditions in the East Anglian countryside in search of butterflies and birds' eggs.

The surname Frohawk is a most unusual one in Britain and has now been lost from the Brisley Hall line, as Frederick and Francis only had daughters, while brother William never married. I rather suspect that the name and family were originally of Dutch origin, since there has long been movement between East Anglia and The Netherlands across the North Sea. Also, photographs of F. W. Frohawk show a rather Continental type of face and posture.

In spite of coming from a fairly large family, Frohawk seems to have spent a good deal of time on his own. Perhaps his brothers and sisters lacked his patience and single-minded approach to the study of natural history and, indeed, he was the one who went furthest in his achievements. A number of other countryside writers and naturalists – among them the Reverend Gilbert White, W. H. Hudson and Edward Thomas – also came from large families, but at the same time were rather solitary in their pursuits, going off on their own into the countryside to study natural history. Although Frohawk's interest in natural history was encouraged by his mother, Frohawk's daughter, Valezina, has recalled that he spoke of his father's concern over his decision to turn the hobby of natural history and drawing into a career.

As a child Frohawk was not thought to be very strong; he was ill with typhoid when he was in his early teens and virtually lost the sight of one eye. This must have put considerable strain on the other eye over the long hours and many years of illustrating in such fine detail. Children with health problems in Victorian times were usually discouraged from taking part in active sport and were often educated at home; many turned to books and serious study of an academic subject, which was not infrequently natural history.

Frohawk's early childhood and formative years were spent in the elegant and spacious surroundings of Brisley Hall which was steeped in history. The family were accustomed to a comfortable and luxurious life-style, with the best of everything as a matter of course. His father was a gentleman farmer who mixed socially in the area and used to shoot with his titled neighbours. As a boy, therefore, Frohawk was used to mixing with the aristocracy and sharing their life-style. He maintained his contact with them during his impoverished years of early manhood when, after a privileged and secure childhood, the family fortune changed and he had to face financial hardship and insecurity.

Although his father was of a genial nature and devoted to his family, he seemed to put his head in the sand over the erosion of the family capital. The landed gentry were rarely trained for a profession and, through the nature of their upbringing, were not well adapted to cope with financial hardship. Frederick Frohawk, however, although clearly looking back nostalgically at his Brisley Hall childhood and regretting the events which denied him such a future, proved to be hard-working and resilient. His consuming interest in natural history and illustrating provided him with a firm structure and purpose in life. He used his natural talents as an artist, naturalist and popular writer to provide a career and basic livelihood.

This did not bring him the sort of income to live in the style in which he had been brought up, but Frohawk had well-established priorities which, along with his interests, helped him to accept the change of fortune. As a naturalist he was able to derive great pleasure from the natural world, something which can be indulged in at no cost. His brother William was less outward-going and was looked after by the old family nurse, Emily, until he died at Balham. Will did not seem to have a career; he looked after animals, particularly dogs which he boarded, but it is not known how he functioned financially.

During his long life, stretching from mid-Victorian times to the end of the Second World War, Frohawk saw great changes in the world around him, and it is fascinating to have a window on the world of over 100 years ago through his first-hand accounts. During the last few years of his life, Frohawk wrote down these recollections in a notebook and they have never previously been studied or published. Throughout this book are selections from these writings, giving a first-hand impression of the times and telling part of his story in his own words. This story has the varied ingredients of home life, countryside, natural history, art, societies, museums, zoos, publishing, writing and history. It follows Frohawk's development into a fine naturalist, artist and writer who held an important place at the hub of the British natural history scene for the duration of a lifetime, from the late nineteenth century to mid-twentieth century.

1
East Anglian Childhood

BRISLEY HALL

Many naturalists can trace their interest in the subject back to earliest childhood and Frohawk is no exception. Living in the East Anglian countryside he was surrounded by rich wildlife, which always intrigued and delighted him. Frohawk's special interest in butterflies and moths also had an early beginning.

My first recollections when a very young child, i.e. before the age of three years, [were] when I remember standing on my mother's hand to look out of the dining-room window, to gaze at a 'Pickcheese' (Blue-titmouse) on a wall apricot tree. My next early observation was climbing upon a chair to reach a match-box on a small chest of drawers to peer inside to see if a gooseberry moth had emerged from a chrysalis, and I remember saying 'when I am three I shan't have to stand on a chair to see if it has turned'. I also can recall my mother taking me into the garden one evening and pointing to the sky where she saw the comet, the year before I was born. In 1867 I was much interested by a weasel which scuttled from beneath a heap of leaves, and a shrew (locally called a 'ranny-mouse') which I tried to catch in a mousetrap. In an adjoining water-meadow where snipe used to breed, I was taken one evening to hear 'The Evening Lamb' as the drumming of the snipe was called. The Quail then nested in a nearby field, and how I admired the richly spotted eggs. In August 1868 I looked with wonderment at a great Convolvulus Hawk Moth which my father found at rest on a gate-post. On a dry bank were a number of lizards (locally called effets) and were considered by the rustics as very poisonous. In the winter of 1867 I was interested in a small flock of Waxwings which visited some larch trees in the plantation at the end of the garden. In the same plantation a nest of the locally so called 'Beebird' (Long-tailed tit). Other local names of birds were 'King Harry', 'Red-cap' (Goldfinch), 'Blood Alf' (Bullfinch), 'Draw-water' (Redpoll), 'Goolie' (Yellow Hammer) and 'Fulfer' (Fieldfare).

How vividly I remember one morning in August 1868 when I first saw a lovely Pale Clouded Yellow butterfly at rest on a dandelion blossom in our pasture, armed with a very primitive butterfly net, the

> ring of a crinoline-steel, bound to a hazel branch, and the bag made of
> a muslin curtain. I dropped on my knees and stealthily crept up to the
> butterfly and suddenly plopped the net over it, greatly to my intense
> joy. I instinctively seemed to realise the rarity of my capture. Many
> years after I learnt this species was numerous in the South and East
> coasts that year when a large migration took place.

Frohawk was to experience other invasions of this migrant butterfly in 1877.

From these earliest recollections we can detect an interest in natural history on the part of young Frohawk's parents, particularly his mother who made a point of showing him things of interest when he was very small. She clearly laid the foundations of the observant nature that characterised the whole of Frohawk's later life and career as a naturalist and artist.

Brisley Hall, Frohawk's first home, had its own special atmosphere, and various recollections of small detail regarding it remained in his mind when writing nearly eighty years later:

> I remember as a child in the mid-sixties smelling these little yellow
> flowers [sweet scented musk], of several plants, kept on the long
> window-seat of the antique landing of Brisley Hall, to scent the house
> with the sweet perfume, a common custom in houses in the past.

The hunting and shooting activities of the country house necessitated a considerable knowledge of the behaviour and habits of animals and birds. This background contributed much to Frohawk's development as a naturalist and later as a popular writer in the country newspaper *The Field*, where natural history was a by-product of the sporting life so much in vogue in the nineteenth century. Conservation was still to make its début on the natural history scene.

GREAT YARMOUTH

In September 1868, when Frohawk was seven, the family left Brisley Hall to live at Great Yarmouth for the next three years in order to be close to the yacht which his father had acquired. Frohawk recalls the move:

> In the autumn of 1868 we left Brisley Hall with its moat and primitive
> surroundings, and many hundred acres of sporting land almost
> adjoining Elmham Hall, the country seat of the late Lord Sondes,
> with whom my father used to hunt and shoot. I recalled seeing quite a
> few white varieties of the old English Pheasant, or Black-necked
> Pheasant (*Phasianus colchicus*) there. I still have a specimen well set up
> by the village bird-stuffer John Elmer of Elmham.

There was much to observe from the new home at Great Yarmouth and also the opportunity to experience the atmosphere of a coastal town and the wonders of the sea and shore.

> When I first saw the sea in 1868 and the ships in the Yarmouth 'Roads' (as the sea off the coast was called) it much interested me, and I soon learned the different rigs of the vessels with the assistance of my elder brother, who was just home on holiday from the training ship *Worcester*.
>
> The first Monday morning, after our arrival, a stiff gale was whistling round the house, upon looking out at sea, I was amazed to see a *great* full-rigged ship driven ashore, only about 200 yds. from the house. What gave me the most intense surprise was the apparent enormous size of the vessel in comparison to the small size of the ships as they appeared to be out at sea two or three miles from the shore which I did not realize.

The latter incident shows Frohawk beginning to discover perspective for himself at a remarkably early age – a concept which was to be very important to him in his later career.

> This great ship the *Hanna Peterson* with the old fashioned painted black and white ports, was laden with coal, apparently, as I remember that when she became a total wreck, for months after the water around her was black with coal-dust . . .
>
> During the winter gales, wrecks were of frequent occurrence, one day in 1869 there were as many as five ships driven ashore. Three were close together, a barque and a brig were between the Britannia Pier and Wellington Pier, and another brig on the other side of the latter, also a barque and a schooner were wrecked on the Scroby Sands off Yarmouth. Except a few tugs, there were in those days a dearth of steamers . . .
>
> The Yarmouth fishing smacks, and Luggers, were wonderfully sea-worthy, the former were usually away for 6 or 7 weeks at a stretch, fishing in the North Sea. In rough weather the men had no opportunity of even taking off their sea-boots, a tougher man than a North Sea Fisherman could not be found . . .
>
> My father owned a very good yacht the *Florence Nightingale* of lateen rig, both sea-worthy and fast, a winner of the Yarmouth Regatta . . .

This yacht was the reason for the family moving to Yarmouth and probably one of the reasons for the financial difficulties which beset the family a few years later. As well as enjoying life on the coast, the Frohawk family also explored the waterways

Lithographic print that Frohawk made in 1890. Many of his early book and journal illustrations were lithographs, made by drawing on a stone block, a technique much used in the nineteenth century.

of the Norfolk Broads at a wonderful time before they became popular with tourists and when the Broads teamed with birds and wildlife. Later, Frohawk prepared illustrations showing the depletion of wildlife from the Broads during his lifetime.

> In those years the now popular Norfolk Broads were [not] then open to the public, and were only visited by a very few, perhaps by a quiet fishing party and a gentle sailing Wherry on the river, no rowdy and fashionable boating parties to upset the peace and quietude as now prevails. We used then to spend a whole week or more up the rivers and broads, enjoying the sights by day, and sounds by night of the birds and beasts. It was on the edge of a marsh by the bank of the river Bure where I first saw a 'Willie-the-Wisp' which fascinated me much. As did the large Heronry that existed in Fritton Park. Also I was much interested in a very large pike (I think 32 lbs.) caught in Oulton Broad. It had a wonderful set of teeth which appeared to be as big as Greyhound's canines.

The will-o'-the-wisp is defined as a lantern or light at night. Various animals, and sometimes plants, are luminescent and are the basis of the legend. In the *Proceedings of the South London Entomological and Natural History Society* (1922–23), K.G. Blair put forward the suggestion that the ghost swift moth is the common source of this phenomenon.

These excursions along the Broads extended young Frohawk's knowledge and experience of birds and other aspects of natural history, but his early involvement with insects was far from forgotten.

> During the year 1870 great invasions of migratory insects occurred at Yarmouth. In all parts of the town the Humming Bird Hawk Moth swarmed. It might commonly be seen buzzing outside windows attracted by geranium blossoms. A vast swarm of Ladybirds in countless millions invaded the district, so great were their numbers that I remember seeing them being swept up into heaps on the Britannia Pier and then swept over into the sea, covering the water with large red patches.
>
> In those days Yarmouth was a comparatively small and quiet seaside resort. The north denes extended from the piers as an untouched stretch of natural ground, with its clumps of furze bushes and growth of coarse grass, the resort of many birds, rabbits and various insects. Flocks of Snow Buntings, locally known as 'Snow Birds' frequented the denes during the winters. When I again visited the place in October 1911, I found it all converted into buildings and a promenade bordering the beach but frequenting the latter I was pleased to see a flock of Snow Birds, where I saw them forty years before. In those years the denes provided a happy hunting ground for me, as I found various insects of much interest to my young mind. I

still have, what I considered then as a curious trophy, a beetle with roots of grass passing through its body. The specimen though 70 years old, is as perfect as when found. I used to spend many hours by the targets at the north Battery on the denes, picking up different things when the rifle and cannon practice had taken place, copper fuses, bullets and the parchment cartridge cases for muskets were interesting to me.

Little boys love to see a fight and the young Frohawk was no exception. Here he recalls one he watched on the beach at Yarmouth.

In 1869 I saw the first fight of my early days, which ended a quarrel between two beachmen over a hole in a herring-net. It happened on Yarmouth beach, the men apparently badly matched, one a big powerful looking fellow known by the name of 'Bob Larne' and a very much shorter man called 'Jimmy Ducks' who evidently got much the worst of the encounter by the appearance of his face, and his blue serge jumper was also freely decorated with blood. I was attracted to the scene by seeing their arms flying about like wind-mill sails. It was soon after this, I beheld a man being dragged ashore, he had been in the water for some time. What interested me was when he was hauled up and turned over, a lot of shrimps and small crabs emerged from his ears and mouth . . .

IPSWICH

In 1871 the family moved once more, probably to acquire new moorings for the yacht, this time to Ipswich, further south on the Suffolk coast. This move provided fresh territory for Frohawk to explore and new things to discover in the natural history field. Their new home, Colwell House, was opposite the arboretum, and Frohawk took an interest in the trees. They were a novelty after the open and comparatively treeless landscape at Yarmouth and provided valuable cover for birds and insects which he found equally fascinating. He was also attracted to the diverse nature of the countryside, with heathland, woods, meadows, marsh and river habitats in their natural state with 'real country lanes unspoilt by the builder'.

Frohawk's daughter, Valezina, recalls that she visited Colwell House with her parents in the late 1920s or early 1930s: It was a large, elegant, white house set in substantial grounds, and she remembers her father saying that it had not changed.

At this time, at the age of eleven, Frohawk made some drawings of old buildings in Ipswich (now exhibited in the Ipswich museum). These early pieces show the high level of skill which Frohawk had already acquired in drawing. Much of his time, however, was still taken up by natural history pursuits.

A pencil drawing of The Royal Oak in Ipswich that Frohawk made at the age of eleven. It is one of a series which are now in the Ipswich Museum. It is most likely that this would have been copied from one of the old prints of Ipswich commonly available at the time.

It was in April 1872 when I first caught a Large Tortoiseshell which was resting on a dry road with wings expanded enjoying the warmth of the April sunshine after its 8 months winters sleep. Arriving home at noon with my relished prize, I beheld a Holly Blue fluttering around a lilac in bloom. This I likewise added to my meagre collection, and the next month I found to my joy a fine Lime Hawk Moth. But it was in July 1872 I first saw the great Fritillaries sucking the nectar from bramble blossoms, and thistles, in Old Hall Wood, Bentley nr. Ipswich, a rich locality for butterflies and moths. When I again visited the wood in July 1881, I found all kinds of butterflies quite abundant. As many as five Purple Emperors I watched playing about around the top of a large oak. The White Admiral was in abundance everywhere, also were the Fritillaries. One large bed of thistles was alive with the High Brown Fritillary. After 35 more years I went to the wood to investigate if suitable as a nature reserve at the suggestion of the late Hon. Charles Rothschild, and found the wood and surroundings unchanged in every respect. Old broken down railings and limbs of trees were lying about as formerly and butterflies were enjoying the rays of sunshine which enlivened the scene between the rain-showers. By the edge of a brook running through a meadow bordering the wood, in the distance I saw something black on the herbage, upon closer investigation, it was a very large brood of fully grown Peacock caterpillars between 300 and 400 spread out in a long mass on *Wild Hop* which was growing along the bank. The caterpillars presented quite an unusual spectacle all scintillating in the sun's rays. This is the only occasion I have found Peacock caterpillars living on hop. The normal food plant is stinging nettle.

I may here allude to the remarkable abundance of the now comparatively rare butterfly the Large Tortoiseshell. In 1872–3 at Ipswich, it was to be seen everywhere. In the spring the females were flying around the elms laying their eggs on the topmost branches or flying about the withered beech leaves where they apparently had been hibernating. During the spring and summer they were commonly seen sitting on tree trunks with expanded wings in the sun. In 1881 I wrote to an old collector Garrett Garrett residing at Ipswich, asking him if the Large Tortoiseshell was still common in the district. His reply was that he had not seen a single specimen since 1873. This is a striking instance of how insects can suddenly disappear without any

*A pencil drawing of a female holly blue (*Celastrina argiolus*). This is the blue butterfly that is most likely to frequent gardens. Its numbers seem to fluctuate in cycles, being common for several years and then scarce. Frohawk reported the presence of the holly blue in gardens of the London suburbs.*

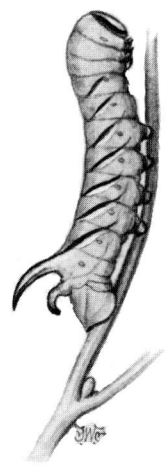

An abnormal caterpillar of the privet hawk moth (Sphinx ligustri) *showing two projections on its tail; the only other similar specimen of which Frohawk was aware was that in Lord Walsingham's collection. The specimen was sent to Frohawk for comment and this fine pencil drawing was done to illustrate his paper in* The Entomologist *in 1930.*

Privet hawk moth from life.

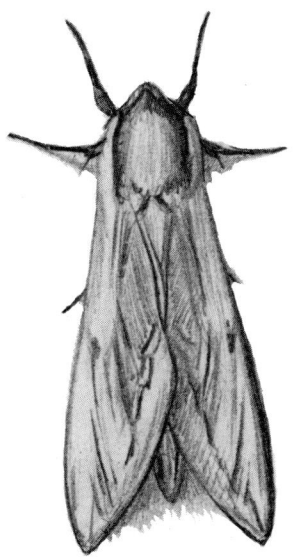

apparent cause except due to migration. I think it may be interesting to allude to the excessive abundance of Hawk Moth caterpillars in Yarmouth seventy years ago chiefly those of the Privet Hawk and Poplar Hawk. They were to be found practically on every plant of Privet in gardens and elsewhere and the poplar trees had their quota of caterpillars all over the neighbourhood. The caterpillars were also numerous in the Ipswich district.

Frohawk developed his observation of natural history whilst living in the contrasting places of East Dereham, inland, and Yarmouth and Ipswich on the coast; all places that yielded some rich collecting sites. He occasionally returned to visit East Anglia in later life and maintained an active interest in the area. In 1940 he was persuaded by Claude Morley (the naturalist and entomologist) to join the Suffolk Naturalists: even at his then advanced age, Frohawk made a number of contributions to their *Transactions*.

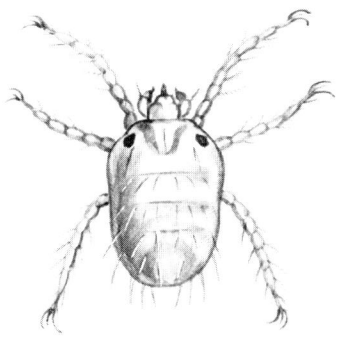

2
Croydon and a Career

Around the 1870s, the family gave up Brisley Hall, and it was also around this time that Frohawk's father died, leaving the family assets eroded to the point of extinction as a result of his affluent lifestyle. It is not known why they decided to settle in Croydon, Surrey, in September 1873, and Frohawk at any rate did not relish the move.

> Once again we changed residence to live in Croydon, which was against my liking, having to leave a fine country house, with all the natural surroundings, the grounds and gardens being the resort of various birds and insects.

Frohawk was to remain in the Home Counties of Surrey, Essex and Kent for the rest of his life. He was, over the next seventy years, to witness great changes as London expanded and many of his earlier haunts and collecting sites were lost under bricks and mortar, while villages of character lost their identity in the amorphous mass of suburbia which came to envelop them. Frohawk's recollections provide interesting accounts of the Home Counties before this expansion.

> In those past days . . . Croydon was then an old fashioned country town, with a population of some 70,000 which has risen at the present time [1940] to about 200,000. The built up area from the S.W. to the N.E. then extended to Waddon and South Croydon Railway Station. It was the northern parts of the town where the buildings extended to Thornton Heath, Norwood and Addiscombe, but these places were more or less isolated by meadows and other open spaces. Beddington one mile from Croydon was in the 'seventies' a small rural hamlet, with its fine old church and noted lych-gate, the old Rectory, a few cottages, the ancient snuff mills by the river Wandle winding through the very picturesque park, and teaming with trout. The Wandle trout were much sought after for stocking other waters, being of choice quality. A little further on at the village of Carshalton, where the river formed a very pretty sheet of water by the roadside, was then public for fishing. I tried a tempting bait for trout and was quickly rewarded with a fine 18 oz. trout one summer morning in 1876. One evening in 1883, a friend journeyed from Chatham on the express purpose to see the Wandle trout. I accompanied him to the big flour-mills which stood at the side of a large sheet of water which was then frequented

23

by various waterfowl, from this lake a clear stream ran to the west. From where we stood on a small bridge spanning the stream, we counted over 200 trout peacefully lying on the gravelly bottom, the water being of crystal clearness gave us a perfect view of a delightful scene. My friend expressed his amazement at seeing so many fish together and under such advantageous conditions.

The friend Frohawk refers to here was John Wood, brother of the zoological artist T.W. Wood.

It was in 1875, whilst living at Croydon, that Frohawk caught typhoid fever – a waterborne disease not uncommon in those days and which also affected his brother and sisters.

The epidemic was traced to the water supply being at the lower part of the town, the water works were therefore moved to the higher ground of the Shirley district.

In 1876 the Frohawk family moved once more to live at South Norwood not far from Croydon which was, at that time, close to green fields and interesting wildlife. With his early interest in butterflies, the following summer, 1877, was particularly memorable to Frohawk for the great invasion of the clouded yellow and was generally known to lepidopterists as the 'edusa' year, after the earlier specific name of this butterfly.

I remember then these beautiful insects fluttering over the clover blossoms growing by the roadsides and fields all over the district.

That year also saw Frohawk's initiation into field sport and he handled a gun for the first time. He proved an efficient marksman and preserved the skins of two of the birds shot on that first occasion. When staying with Admiral Charlewood in Devon in 1878, Frohawk went shooting again and successfully shot a ring plover on a mud-flat at seventy-two yards. On the same trip, sailing in the Bristol Channel, he shot a shearwater, guillemot and razorbill. Some of his water colour studies on birds used those he had shot.

Frohawk was educated at Norwood College, but his schooling was interrupted by illness from typhoid and in his teens he suffered from serious outbreaks of hay fever, a condition which was to afflict him for forty years.

In 1880 there was another move of house, this time from South Norwood to Upper Norwood, and it was during this period that Frohawk worked especially hard developing his skills in drawing and undertaking his first regular commissions to illustrate magazines (*The Field*) and other publications for members of staff at the British Museum. Spare time was spent walking, on long solitary expeditions into the nearby countryside to study wildlife and collect information for pictures.

Frohawk on a shooting excursion. Like many countrymen of his time he enjoyed shooting, but he used the gun sparingly and mostly to procure birds as specimens for illustration and scientific study. Some of his bird sketches are annotated 'shot F.W.F.' followed by the date.

At this time Frohawk did many oil paintings of wildlife and landscape, which were exhibited locally and soon found ready customers. Most of the early Frohawk oil paintings of the 1880s are now scattered and their present whereabouts are unknown. A few were retained in the family and are now in the ownership of Frohawk's daughter Valezina, apart from some which she has given to museums.

In 1881 I painted a picture in oils depicting a winter scene of Hooded Crows and a dead lamb life size. As I was anxious to get an accurate picture of a lamb, I heard of some early black-faced lambs being born on the Archbishop of Canterbury's estate at Addington Palace and knowing his steward, I called there on January 21st and found a lamb of a week old had just died, therefore it was just what I wanted, so with it under my arm walked the five miles home. The lamb attracted the attention of the police, and little boys. This picture was exhibited in London, it was bought and hung between two pictures by Landseer in the Gallery of a Mansion at Bishop's Stortford.

Still life study of a pot plant which Frohawk painted in oils in 1876 when he was fifteen. The gold-laced polyanthus on the ground was a popular garden plant in the nineteenth century and earlier.

*Evening in the woods near Addington, Surrey, 1881. Oil painting by
Frohawk recently presented to the National Museum of Wales, Cardiff.
Many other oil paintings of countryside scenes in the Croydon area were made
about this time, but they were sold at exhibitions and their present ownership is
unknown.*

When he could, Frohawk took the opportunity of walks in the country, and it was
in 1884 that he did the longest walk of his life:

> In August 1884 I took a long walk of exactly 48 miles, my longest walk
> in a day, leaving at 8.30 a.m., arriving home at 8.30 p.m., stopping for
> lunch at 1 p.m. which consisted of a sea-biscuit and ½ pint of ale. On
> another occasion I walked 42 miles one night, the 15th September
> 1883, leaving home at 10.20 p.m. arriving home at 8.30 a.m. It was a
> brilliant fine night with a full moon. I met only 7 people in the country
> districts, two of these were men asleep with a dog between them under
> a hedge, and two were evidently burglars, as I noticed them emerge
> from the front of a large white house in the Wallingham district, I
> think it was 'Beech Farm'. They had bulging sacks on their backs and

something soft on their feet, it was 2 a.m. During that still autumn night I only heard the Lapwings passing over, a Tawny Owl hooting and a long-eared bat. At 5.30 a.m. I watched a mole hunting amongst a strip of grass beside the road, probably catching the 'early worm'.

FINANCIAL HARDSHIPS

Although their lifestyle was not so luxurious after the family's departure from East Anglia, in his memoir Frohawk does not give any impression that he was aware of financial problems until after they had been in Croydon for ten years. Then, in spring 1884 the carefree life without responsibilities, with a comfortable home background and time to indulge in interests came abruptly to an end. Frohawk does not go into the detailed causes of this in his memoir, although the sudden change of lifestyle and lack of financial security affected him, coming as it did at the beginning of his career as an illustrator. The financial troubles alluded to were probably connected with his father overspending and leaving debts to be cleared when he died.

Frohawk often drew domestic animals, like these chickens, at the Crystal Palace shows. This is an early working sketch in pencil, November 1880.

In April 1884 financial trouble befell the family therefore we left Upper Norwood. Being the only one capable of earning anything, having by then published a few drawings in *The Field* and made several sketches of the exhibits at the Crystal Palace shows, I fortunately had made a start and turned my nature study to some use, although it was generally ridiculed by most at home. I persevered with it, going alone to the silent fields and woods for the day, learning what I could about the wonderful secrets of nature, made me contented and happy, the other members of the family being regardless of my solitary doings, until the fateful April of 1884. So 'taking the Bull by the horns' I put in my best to do what I could to 'keep the wolf from the door' as hard as it was to turn from luxury to absolute poverty through no fault of ones-self. Having a most precious, devoted and loving invalid mother, and sisters to provide for (with no help from relatives) and a brother who was unable to be of much assistance I had to struggle hard. I rented a little cottage for her in the country just 20 miles from the rooms (two) taken for my brother and self in a little street at New Cross for cheapness. Two rooms and board 13/6 per week for both. For 8 months kept well on scanty food.

To save the rail fare, Frohawk walked to Eltham and back every other weekend to visit his mother and sisters. Mrs Frohawk lived in the Eltham cottage for over two years before she died in 1887, and during that time her artist son came to know the Kent countryside at weekends.

In 1887 the cottage was given up for a house rented in Balham, South London to serve as a home for the two brothers and two sisters. Although Frohawk moved after he married, his brother Will remained at Balham for the rest of his life. Will, whom his niece Valezina remembers as a pleasant man, was also keen on animals and practised as a canine specialist, but he had no qualifications and seemed to lack the perseverance of his more industrious brother Frederick, on whose shoulders the financial welfare of the family depended. This was a time of extremely hard work during which Frohawk was able to keep going from the stamina of his youth, whilst clearly burning the candle at both ends.

> I was then fully occupied with work chiefly at the British Museum, figuring by lithography Typical specimens of Lepidoptera for Dr. A.G. Butler [Keeper of Entomology at the museum]. I was also commissioned to illustrate (many litho plates of) lepidoptera from China and Korea for Mr. John Leech. As these were required at once, I had to do this work at night starting at 6.30 p.m. and working by lamp light, until 2.30 a.m. and the museum work in the day; this day and night work I carried on without a break (except Sundays when the museum was closed) for exactly 150 days and nights.

These illustrations were published in the *Proceedings of the Zoological Society of London*.

Sunflower in a Japanese vase, 1831. A studio still life oil painting that has recently been presented by Frohawk's daughter to the National Museum of Wales, Cardiff. The fine carved chest on which the vase stands used to belong to Lord Nelson whose home was also in Norfolk, and the chest was given by him to the Frohawk family.

WILDLIFE IN LONDON

Being now under pressure from a heavy programme of commissioned artwork, largely to support his brother and sisters, Frohawk had little opportunity for the long country walks of his youth. Instead, he turned his attentions to the immediate surroundings of the South London commons and has left us valuable accounts of the changes which led to the demise of their wildlife as London spilled beyond its former boundaries.

Previous to the early nineties of last century, Balham and the surrounding district was very different from what it presents at the present time. Therefore I think it may be of some interest to give some rough idea of the various creatures which I met with on Tooting Common (Balham) during the years 1887 to 1894 inclusive, which was then a small piece of natural ground adjoining unspoilt country; but early in the 90s it was levelled and otherwise 'improved' by the authorities, greatly to the regret of the nature lovers and students of the fauna and flora of the district. This exterminated many nesting birds and various other creatures, which had enjoyed a congenial resort amid the former varied vegetation.

Respecting the mammals I observed were the stoat, weasel, rabbit, red squirrel, hedgehog, mole, common shrew, field vole, long-tailed field mouse, rat and three species of bats.

A very interesting and extremely local inhabitant of the common, was the natterjack toad, I often saw them running mouse-like, to take cover in the rough growth surrounding the pond as I approached their haunts. The birds which frequented the common seen by myself amounted to 75 species, of these 41 nested there or the immediate surroundings. I also often came across the common lizard and the slow worm. I may add that Tooting Common is only 5 miles from Charing Cross. It was a great relaxation to take an hours observation of the creatures haunting the common.

The natterjack toad, once more widespread in Britain, is today an endangered species receiving special protection under the Wildlife and Countryside Act. This handsome toad, recognised by a conspicuous yellow stripe down its back, breeds in shallow pools that have a tendency to dry out too quickly for the completion of the tadpoles' development. The tidying up of the countryside, filling in small pools, ponds, puddles and ditches, has largely destroyed breeding sites for this now rare toad, but it was not uncommon locally in the early part of Frohawk's lifetime when he recorded them on Tooting Common. The decline started in about 1900.

Frohawk's account of the birds of Tooting Common was published in *The Zoologist* in 1894.

  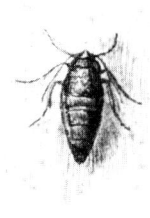

*Pencil sketch of the pale brindléd beauty (*Apocheima pilosaria*) made in 1881 when Frohawk was twenty. The moth is on the wing early in the year and in daytime it sits on tree-trunks and fence palings. It is generally distributed in the British Isles.*

Among the various kinds of Insects which came under notice a few are worth alluding to. In 1880 a Camberwell Beauty was captured while at rest on the trunk of an old elm on August 19th and another was taken ten days later on the Brixton Rd, a short distance away. Again on August 6th 1887 I saw a beautiful specimen flying over a freshly watered road, only a few feet away close to the common. Also another was seen shortly afterwards flying between the platforms of Balham Station.

Some exciting butterfly rarities occasionally turned up in the garden at Dornton Road, Balham.

In 1893 the dry and hot summer, in July, I was carrying a potted up plant of violet containing a Silver-washed Fritillary var. *valezina*[1], enclosed with a gauze cover, upon which syrup was spread as food for the butterfly. The syrup attracted a beautiful Large Tortoiseshell which floated down and settled on my arm. This happened in my garden at Balham. I allude to this incident because this butterfly after the nineties gradually became rarer, and is still looked upon as an uncommon species, only occasionally turning up in different counties, probably due to migration . . .

In 1893 there were countless numbers of the Small Copper on the common, and in August of that year, I found an egg of the Clouded Yellow laid upon one of the leaves of a clover plant that I dug up (to pot up) for the purpose of placing a female Clouded Yellow upon to obtain eggs from her. After a few days she laid between 200 and 300.

[1]*Now regarded as a form rather than a variety.*

32

> In those days the Lime Hawk Moth was very abundant in the district, as well as a large number of species more or less uncommon. Tooting Common then offered opportunities for various nature studies, both respecting the Fauna and Flora.

Many of the haunts where Frohawk studied natural history in South London have long since been built on or tidied up, particularly with the advent of machinery to keep grass closely and evenly mown, thus reducing the diversity of plant and animal species. With the spread of London and vast areas of high-density urban housing, all relying on coal for heating, the air steadily became more polluted with soot and sulphurous gases and, as a result, the more interesting species of mosses, liverworts and lichens disappeared. London's air has now been improved following clean air Acts and in the 1980s a great interest has developed in urban wildlife through television and environmental education projects. Many people have come to realise that tidy urban parkland has limited scope for wildlife, while a great variety of plants and animals have adapted to living on abandoned wasteground. Animals like the fox, starling and gulls find a livelihood in human waste and their numbers are on the increase.

Societies such as the South London Entomological and Natural History Society (now called the British Entomological and Natural History Society), the London Natural History Society and the Croydon Natural History and Scientific Society have always taken an interest in London's wildlife, but most of their field meetings were to places in the nearby countryside. There is now a new London Wildlife Trust which functions as a conservation body for London.

The contrast between Frohawk's notes on wildlife in London and the modern situation are striking. Red squirrels no longer occur in Lloyd Park, Croydon, having long since been replaced with the introduced grey squirrel. Frohawk's writings are now a most valuable indication of what existed there over a century ago, much of which has now been lost.

CLOSE CALLS

During Frohawk's time in Surrey and South London up to his marriage, he was involved in various accidents which could have had serious consequences but from which he was saved.

In 1878 a friend accidentally let off a shooting stick gun and the shot blew up inches from Frohawk's left foot, just avoiding crippling him for life. The same year, whilst ice skating at the Crystal Palace, Frohawk was going at full speed and was about to turn when another skater pushed him in the back causing him to crash into the wall at the end of the rink, hitting it with the crown of his head. He was led home in a dazed state, but otherwise unhurt.

In August 1885 Frohawk recorded escaping from a bull whilst collecting butterflies at Cudham, Surrey. On seeing the bull charge in his direction he bolted uphill and scaled some iron railings just in time. Even butterfly collecting can be hazardous!

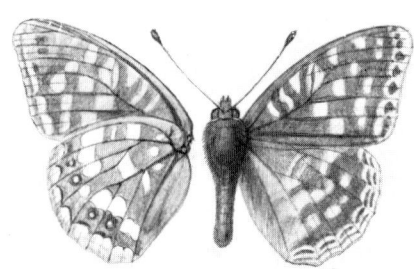

3

Frohawk at Home

MARRIAGE TO MARGARET

On 5 June 1895, when he was 33, Frederick Frohawk married Margaret Grant who was 27. The wedding took place at Shirley Church near Croydon, which was then in the country. The ceremony was to have been conducted by the Reverend Wilks (known in horticultural circles for developing the unusual Shirley Poppy), but Wilks was ill that day and another vicar had to take his place. Frohawk described it as 'a very happy and quiet wedding. We went direct to my house at Balham, then a peaceful suburb.'

A month later the couple had a honeymoon in the New Forest, a place to which Frohawk returned many times during his long life. For the last week they had as their guest W.B. Tegetmeier, who was the editor of *The Field*, a newspaper to which Frohawk had contributed illustrations and notes for fourteen years. The venerable Tegetmeier represented something of a father figure to Frohawk, having taken the young artist under his wing, giving him his earliest commissions. Typical of naturalists, this honeymoon doubled up as a collecting trip, as did the family holidays in subsequent years when the dates were selected to coincide with peak occurrence of butterflies. The two daughters of this first marriage were born in 1896 and 1898, the latter after they had moved to Bromley, Kent.

After sharing the house at Balham since 1887 the Frohawk brothers and sisters went their own way. The sisters, Lydia and Katharine (Kate), funded by their brother Frederick, went to stay for a while with Margaret Frohawk's sisters in the United States. Will stayed in Balham with the family nurse Emily. On her return to England Lydia married James Linwood-Palmer and settled at Heston, Middlesex. Kate never married and divided her time between the homes of her brother Will and sister Lydia.

Frederick Frohawk had at least seventeen homes in his lifetime and until he was in his mid-sixties he always rented accommodation. This wandering family gravitated around the area on the outskirts of London in Surrey and Kent and into Essex, near Southend.

> From September 1900 to September 1903 we resided at Croydon and left there for Hockley Essex where we lived in a very old charming cottage, until finally living at Rayleigh, staying there till 1911. Rayleigh in those days was an old fashioned village on high ground.

On the mound a picturesque windmill in full working order over-
looked the village, but this interesting land-mark was taken down
about 1907 and the surroundings modernized and spoiled. Before
then the foxhounds used to meet in the High Street.

We have little information about Margaret, although she was Frohawk's compan-
ion on various natural history holidays, including the early visits to the Scilly Isles
where he made a number of bird studies in water-colour, some of which are now in
the British Museum (Natural History). In his memoir he recalled the visit in May
1897 with Margaret and their baby. They stayed in a cottage at St Agnes, and at
night the room was periodically lit by beams from the lighthouse. Frohawk knew
the Governor of the islands, T.A. Dorrien-Smith, who gave him permission to
collect specimens of eggs and birds for study. We will return to his observations on
birds of the Scilly Isles in Chapters 10 and 11.

Margaret evidently shared Frohawk's interest in birds and in February 1897
she contributed a letter to *The Field*:

GREAT GREY SHRIKE AT OXTED

I saw a fine great grey shrike (*Lanius excubitor*) at Oxted, Surrey, on the
6th inst. It looked particularly beautiful and attractive in the way in
which it perched on the top of a hop-pole by expanding its large tail
immediately before perching.

MARGARET FROHAWK

According to Frohawk's only surviving daughter (of his second marriage),
Margaret suffered much from ill health and a weak heart. In 1907, whilst they
were living at Rayleigh, Essex, Margaret died of heart failure and Frohawk was
left a widower with two young girls of nine and eleven to bring up. He married
again a few years later.

MARRIAGE TO MABEL

On 4 October 1911 at St James's, Piccadilly in London, Frohawk married Mabel
Jane Hart Bowman, a friend of the family whom he always called 'Nommie'.

By this time Frohawk had long enjoyed the friendship of the two Rothschild
brothers, Walter (later Lord Rothschild) and Charles, who were both keen
naturalists. He met Walter Rothschild through the British Museum (Natural
History) and through him came to know Charles who invited Frohawk to spend
his second honeymoon at his home.

At the special wish of the late Hon. Charles Rothschild we spent our
honeymoon at his favourite home the old Manor House at Ashton,

a Christmas Carol.

A Christmas card painted in water-colour by Frohawk in 1911 shortly after his second marriage.

Northants, where we spent a very enjoyable twelve days. Everything was made the essence of comfort for our reception and pleasure. It was also his express wish for us to go there whenever we wanted a holiday and were invited to spend the Christmas there in 1912 with my two daughters. We all had a most enjoyable time.

This second marriage proved very happy as Mabel took such a great interest in his work and used to accompany him in the field. Being many years younger than Frohawk, she died only recently in 1983 and was buried at Selborne, Hampshire.

This marriage caused a move from Essex, and the Frohawk family now took up residence at Stanley House, Park Road in Wallington, Surrey, and it was there that his youngest daughter, Barbara Valezina, was born.

The long walks in the countryside of Surrey and Kent which Frohawk enjoyed during his youth were still his pleasure some thirty years later.

On September 15, 1913 I went for a thirty-two mile walk through Croydon, Addington, Biggin Hill, Leaves Green, Keston, Orpington, Bromley, Shortlands, Beckenham, Penge, Croydon, Waddon and home at Wallington. From Croydon to Bromley was all peaceful

Uplands, Thundersley, Essex, where Frohawk and his family lived from 1917 until 1923. He found great pleasure in the Essex countryside which was rich in natural history.

country – saw swallows chasing a bat in full sunshine, and watched a weasel trying to entice a robin from its perch on an iron railing to the road, but it did not succeed. This was a happy days walk, everything at peace. For two miles along a country lane not a person was to be seen, I only passed an old bob-tailed sheep dog, he went his way and I went mine.

In 1917 Frohawk and family returned to Essex where they rented a house called Uplands in Thundersley near Southend, a place he came to love dearly. At that house he had a study-cum-studio in one of the upstairs rooms which commanded a splendid view across the fields. He used a little brass telescope to watch and draw wildlife from the study window. This is now in the possession of his daughter, Valezina together with some pencil sketches he made there and a notebook on the weather. Frohawk enjoyed the Essex countryside, and Valezina remembers hearing of her father's concern over a new road which was to run across the valley behind the property and would disturb the peace. Frohawk studied the natural history of the area and took part in shooting, a typical country sport of the time.

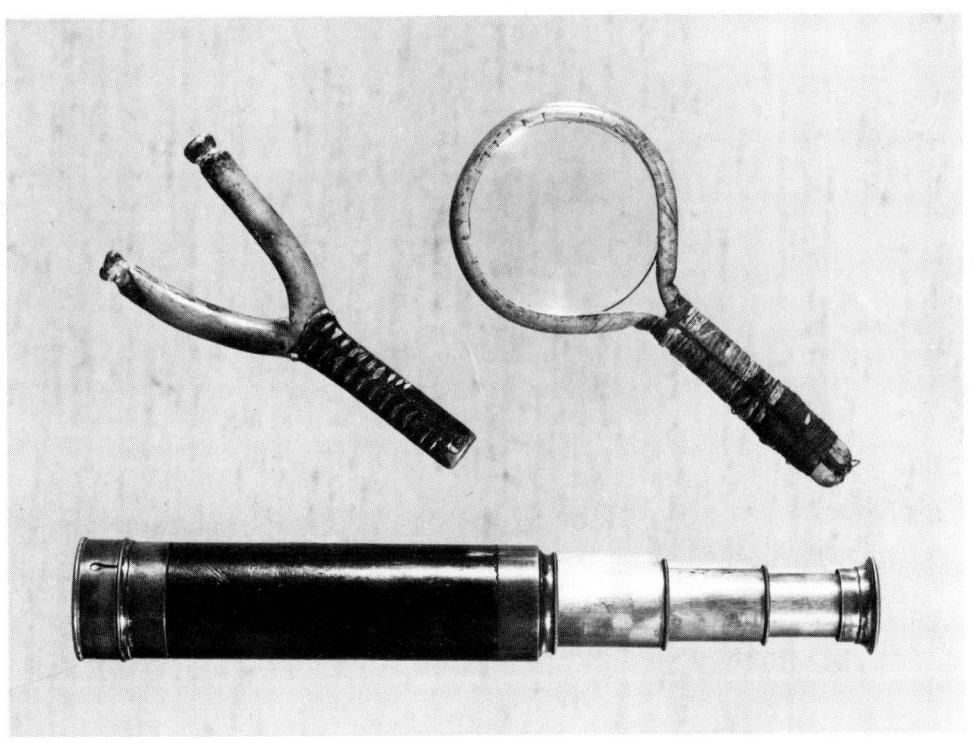

Tools of the trade: Frohawk's brass telescope, magnifying glass and catapult. He found the catapult 'a most useful weapon for collecting small birds'.

> While living at Rayleigh from 1903 to 1911 and Thundersley 1917–
> 1923, with a partner we had about 300 acres of shooting from
> Hockley, other friends took adjoining shoots which amounted to
> about 1,000 acres altogether, principally partridges and Red-legged
> Partridges. I also had a small shoot of 100 acres, snipe, duck,
> partridges and lapwings and golden plover.

For Frohawk the shoot was not entirely sport, for it also provided much useful material for study and drawing.

In 1923 the family had to leave Uplands since the old lady from whom they rented it wished to sell the house and they could not afford at that stage to buy it. The proposed new road in the valley was also a threat. Dr Butler, by this time retired from his post at the British Museum, came to the rescue.

> We left Thundersley in September 1923 to reside at Beckenham with
> my old friend Dr. A.G. Butler until his death in 1925. In September of
> that year we moved to Romney Cottage, Carshalton, Surrey . . .

A pair of red-legged partridges drawn from life as seen through a telescope from the study window at Uplands, 9 March 1919. This pencil drawing was reproduced in The Field.

Beckenham adjoining Penge, a quarter of a century ago is today like other suburban districts, an altered place . . .

Dr Butler was not without eccentricities. As a hobby he kept cage-birds, the subject of some of his books, and at one time his entire house was full of twittering cages, but these had gone by the time the Frohawk family shared the house. After Dr Butler died, the family moved to Carshalton for a few years before settling in 1927 in Sutton, which was to remain Frohawk's home for the rest of his life.

Frohawk bought the house 'Essendene' in Cavendish Road, Sutton, Surrey and this purchase was made possible only by the sale of his butterfly collection to Lord Rothschild. In the possession of his daughter is a sale agreement for 6,000 specimens sold to Lord Rothschild for £1,000 in 1927 to be paid in instalments. The butterfly collection, built up over his lifetime, was one of his most valued possessions and it must have been a considerable sacrifice to part with it, even to such a close friend. However it secured a permanent home for him and his family. His wife Mabel and daughter Valezina continued to live at 'Essendene' after he died, until in the 1960s they sold it and moved to Pulborough in West Sussex. 'Essendene', together with other properties in Cavendish Road, was demolished and the site was redeveloped.

Natural history and artwork filled Frohawk's life to capacity and he was always very busy, but he enjoyed the company of his family and friends and the music-making of Mabel and Valezina, who studied the cello under the world-famous cellist Suggia. Working mostly from home, he was constantly in the company of his wife and daughter who became much involved in his world of natural history. Whilst at Sutton, they belonged to an unofficial group of naturalists who met in each others' houses in rotation.

In *Who was Who* (1941–1950), Frohawk's hobby is recorded as studying natural history, and the little spare time he had away from illustrating and editorial work was often spent observing the behaviour of butterflies. His wife and daughter used to accompany him in the field; Valezina was named after a form of the silver-washed fritillary butterfly (*Argynnis paphia*) and she appears in several family photographs holding a butterfly net. With her auburn hair she was strikingly attractive, and she features in her father's obituary in the *Transactions of the Suffolk Naturalists' Society*:

> With one of them, a beautiful girl with a beautiful name Valezina (who last year married Lord Bolingbroke), him and his second wife, the 'Suffolk quintette' had the pleasure of collecting upon several occasions a decade ago in the New Forest.

The Frohawk family on a day out in the country. Left to right: Mabel Jane Frohawk, Valezina Frohawk and F.W. Frohawk.

Frohawk and his youngest daughter Valezina were always very close. She did not marry until after her father's death and her husband, the late Lord Bolingbroke, was one of her father's entomological contacts.

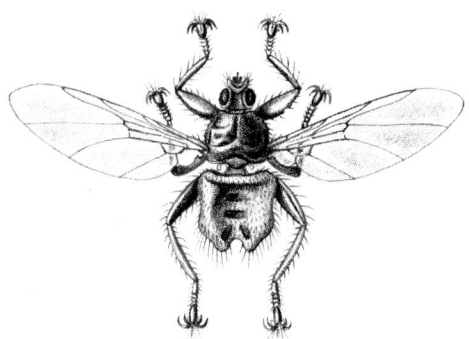

4

Naturalist, Artist and Author

As we have seen from the account of Frohawk's childhood, natural history studies and drawing were among his earliest pursuits. Through considerable practice, he developed great skills as an observant naturalist and artist while still in his boyhood, and it was around these activities that he decided to base his life. As the son of a gentleman farmer his family assumed that his life in the country would revolve around the social activities of shooting and fishing. Although not averse to a little shooting and fishing, Frohawk saw a different future for himself. Together with many boys of a similar background, he attended private schools but did not proceed to university as he was not destined for a career. His later achievements are the more remarkable in that he was self-taught both in art and in biology. In fact, the secure and leisurely life to which he had been brought up was not to last, and he was forced to earn some sort of income without delay.

Frohawk's powers of observation and an eye for accuracy and detail provided a firm foundation for his work as a natural history illustrator. It is clear that he had a natural aptitude for drawing, and this was developed by considerable practice in observing and drawing living animals, often at the zoo, so that he achieved accuracy in both body form, coat markings etc., and also in the posture and general demeanour of the animal.

OIL PAINTINGS

Frohawk's early work consisted mostly of oil paintings, which were sometimes portraits of animals and sometimes countryside scenes. These were exhibited at art shows and, since most of them were sold, their present whereabouts are unknown. His first painting was exhibited when he was only nineteen years old.

> In 1880 an exhibition of paintings was held at the Town Hall, South Norwood. I had just finished an oil painting (36 × 24 inches) of a pair of lions from life (in the Zoo). It gained second prize and soon after was sold for ten guineas, my first picture sold.

*Some of Frohawk's art equipment, including a much-used paint box, porcelain
and wooden palettes and a wooden block drawn for cutting. This is the red
admiral on a thistle that led to Frohawk being commissioned to make
drawings for the British Museum.*

The oil paintings benefited from the considerable drawing skills which Frohawk
had developed during the 1870s, while making practice pencil sketches of animals
at the Zoo and domestic livestock (dogs, cats, chickens, and so on) at the Crystal
Palace shows. The art exhibitions at the Crystal Palace enabled Frohawk to see
the work of other artists and also provided a pitch to display and sell his own
paintings:

> There was a permanent exhibition of pictures which occupied one of
> the main galleries. Some of the pictures were by the noted artists of the
> day. I remember a fine oil painting by Sir Richard Ansdel represent-
> ing a stag and hounds, also another large picture by Heywood Hardy
> of Lions fighting which struck me as a very fine piece of work. There
> was also a very careful picture of sheep wending their way through the
> snow at sundown, the whole picture having a very realistic cold
> atmospheric effect. In 1882 I exhibited a small oil painting of
> Lilies-of-the-Valley in a crackle china vase with a ruby velvet curtain
> background, it quickly found a purchaser.

*Rajah Brooke's birdwing butterfly (*Trogonoptera brookiana*). This oil painting was highly praised by Rowland Trimen, the Curator of the South African Museum at Cape Town, when he met Frohawk at the British Museum in the 1880s. This spectacular tropical butterfly was first discovered in Borneo in 1855 and named after Sir James Brooke, ruler of Sarawak.*

There was, however, at least one butterfly in the early oil paintings:

> It was at the end of the 80's that Dr. Butler, Keeper of entomology at the Museum, introduced me to Rowland Trimen curator of the Capetown Museum, who was then on holiday in England. He being a distinguished entomologist. Dr. Butler showed him an oil painting of mine of a big Bornean butterfly in flight (*Ornithoptera brookiana*) which Trimen considered the finest picture of this great handsome insect he had ever seen.

Once people got to know his work, Frohawk received commissions to prepare pictures of animals.

Honest Tom, a champion shire stallion drawn at Poulton-le-Fylde,
Lancashire, 1885, one of Frohawk's early commissioned drawings.

My second order directly followed, was a large drawing of the
champion shire stallion 'Honest Tom' (also an oil painting I did for
the Cart Horse Society), the property of T.H. Miller of Singleton
Park, Poulton-le-Fylde, Lancs., at whose spacious mansion I stayed.
The great house stood on high ground surrounded by a beautiful park
and lovely views. While there in March 1884, at the stud farm were 30
brood mares, a fine 'fire' goat had the run of the stables. In case of fire
the horses would follow the goat to safety as it had no fear of fire.

Oil paintings steadily gave way to book and journal illustration, but there is a
record of one oil done rather later.

In 1901 I painted in oils a picture entitled 'The Licensed Hawker',
representing a Goshawk and Rabbit life size. This was from a sketch I
made when accompanying the late F.H. Salvin, the great Falconer on
his last days hawking. The picture was exhibited at the Carlton
galleries, London, and was produced as a Xmas supplement to *The*

Field. Odd circumstances occurred regarding this supplement. When my friend Scott Wilson visited a friend of his living in Rio Janera he was interested in seeing this picture in his room there, and when Wilson and myself viewed the empty house to let at Soham, Suffolk we were surprised to see this picture stuck up on a wall of this house, the only thing remaining in the place.

F.H. Salvin used to live at Sutton Place near Guildford, a fine stately home now in the care of a private trust and open to the public.

WATER-COLOURS

Although most of Frohawk's early paintings in the 1880s were in oil, he records doing a large water-colour in 1885:

> Returning to pictures, in 1885 I painted in water colours, a rather effective picture, of an Elephant hunt from a description of one in India. Before it was quite finished a wealthy man bought it to hang beside some 'Lansers' in his picture gallery. This was somewhat encouraging to a comparative beginner.

Frohawk painted various other water-colours, mostly of birds and butterflies, and this medium was used increasingly for his magazine and book illustrations.

Whilst his early paintings were done entirely from his own inspiration, commissioned work and book illustration offered less freedom, both in terms of subject matter and in technique. However, during the early part of Frohawk's career there were advances in the printing process which extended the range of media possible for illustrative work.

WOODCUTS

Frohawk's career as a book illustrator can be said to have begun with his appointment as zoological artist to *The Field* in 1881. From that date until 1890 his drawings for the magazine were done on wooden blocks. Woodcuts are one of the earliest types of book illustration, going right back to the beginnings of printing, and they enjoyed a revival in popularity during the nineteenth century.

The block for a woodcut print is worked on the plank wood, along the grain, so woodcut blocks can be quite large, as were those Frohawk did for *The Field* in the 1880s. In commercial work it was usual for the artist to draw the picture on the block, and then the actual working with a knife to be done by another person, the name of both artist and block cutter appearing on the final print. Although the

Song thrush; a hand coloured print, probably of a wood engraving, although it is larger than usual for this method of print-making. The corners of the print show impressions on the paper made by bearers which give extra support in the press. (Size 23 × 19.25cm.)

original woodcut blocks could be used directly for small runs, it was usual for an electrotype duplicate plate to be made for long runs, such as required by *The Field*. These were prepared by depositing a shell of copper onto a mould of the original block; the resulting metal surface would stand the wear of long print runs better than the wooden block, which would eventually deteriorate with use. The rather crisp images of *The Field* woodcuts are indicative of the electrotype method.

Frohawk refers in his writings to doing preparatory drawings on wood-engraving blocks, and some of these uncut blocks are in the possession of his youngest daughter. The terms 'woodcut' and 'wood engraving' are often used loosely and incorrectly, for they refer to two different techniques of print-making from wooden blocks. The block for wood engraving is worked on the end-grain of a hard, fine textured wood like yew, box or fruitwood. This wood is harder and requires a special tool – a graver – to work it. Large blocks of end-grain wood are difficult and costly to obtain, so wood engravings tend to be smaller in size than woodcuts and, because of the nature of the surface of the block, finer lines and detail are possible. However, in practice it is not always easy to distinguish between a print from a woodcut and a wood engraving, particularly if a woodcut is done carefully on a good quality block.

Whilst most modern wood engravers do their own graving (including the bird artist C.F. Tunnicliffe who worked in this medium from 1930–60) Frohawk evidently did not, probably because printers at the time employed their own block cutters.

The wood engraving technique was developed in the eighteenth century and made popular by the bird artist Thomas Bewick. Frohawk recalls doing some illustrations for wood engraving to be used in the ninth edition of the *Encyclopaedia Britannica*. Although called upon to illustrate a particular animal, he typically prepared a complete picture showing the animal in relation to its surroundings. Tunnicliffe tended to use the same approach with his work.

The Laysan crake (Porzanula palmeri), *a new species of bird described by Frohawk in 1892. These birds with their black chicks were drawn for Walter Rothschild to illustrate his book* The Avifauna of Laysan and the Neighbouring Islands *published in 1893–1900. This is a preliminary water-colour which Frohawk copied on to a stone block for a chromolithograph used in the book.*

LITHOGRAPHY

Another technique in which Frohawk needed to acquire proficiency was lithography, a method of printing from inked stone blocks that was developed in 1798. Being cheaper than the steel engraving which was much used in the eighteenth century, lithography soon came into general use and was still practised in the early days of Frohawk's career. Lithography is a print-making technique which uses a smooth block of fine-grained stone (usually a German limestone) on to which a drawing is made with greasy crayon or litho ink. When the block is printed, only the parts which have been drawn on will take up the ink. Lithography gives a softer picture than steel or wood block methods and some lithographs can be 'woolly'. By using several stone blocks it is possible to do colour printing, a method known as chromolithography, which replaced the individually hand-coloured illustrations of earlier books.

. In some situations the artist provided a drawing that was copied on to the stone by a commercially employed craftsman (or lithographic artist). This is indicated by the abbreviation 'del.' followed by the artist's name and 'lith,' by the lithographer's name, which both appear in small print at the bottom of the illustration. Sometimes, as in Frohawk's case, the artist prepared the drawing in

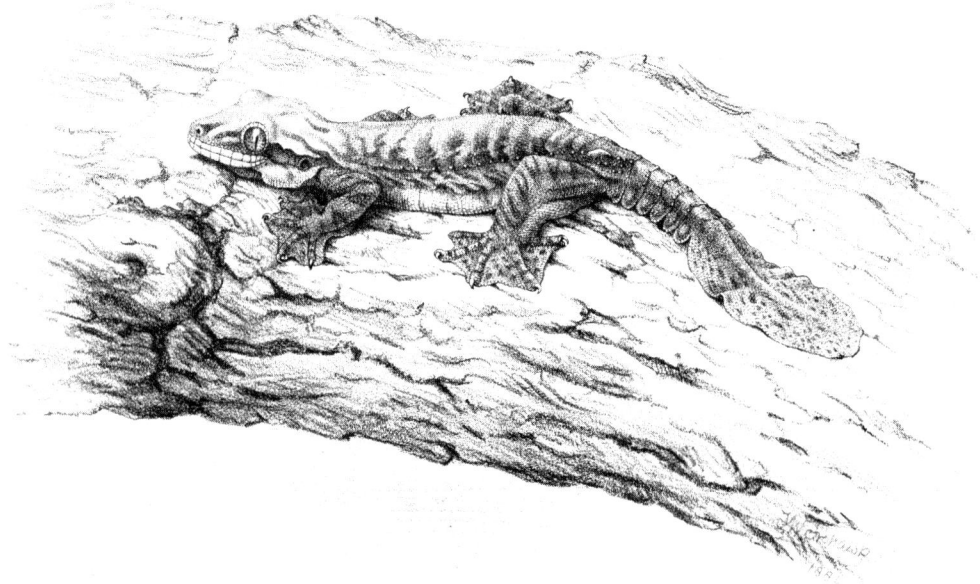

Frohawk's first attempt at lithography in 1884. The success of this print led to commissioned work for Dr Boulenger of the British Museum. This illustration of a flying gecko at London Zoo was also copied on to a wood block and published as a woodcut print in The Field *(1884) to illustrate an article by W.B. Tegetmeier.*

crayon directly on the block; this is an autolithograph or 'del. et lith.' Frohawk described his first work in lithography:

> In 1884 I tried my hand at lithography and obtained the few materials necessary. When the drawing was done I took the stone to be proved (printed) which was quite successful and resulted by Dr. Boulenger (the authority on Reptiles) commissioning me to do a plate for publication in the Proceedings of the Zoological Society.

Frohawk prepared the artwork for many lithographs, which included the illustrations for Edward Bartlett's book *A Monograph of the Weaver Birds and Arboreal and Terrestrial Finches*; Dr Butler's *Foreign Finches in Captivity* (the second edition included chromolithographs) and *British Birds with their Nests and Eggs*; Scott B. Wilson and A.H. Evans's *Aves Hawaiiensis: The Birds of the Sandwich Islands*; Lord Rothschild's *Avifauna of Laysan*; the Russian ornithologist Prince Alpheraky's *The Geese of Europe and Asia*; and G.M. Mathews's *Birds of Norfolk and Lord Howe Islands*. Frohawk's work was also produced as lithographic plates in scientific journals, including *The Entomologist*, *Proceedings of the Zoological Society of London*, *Novitates Zoologicae* (published by Lord Rothschild at Tring) and *The Ibis*.

OTHER METHODS

A new technique of drawing – crayon on coated textured paper – was adopted for illustrations in *The Field* from 1891–98, and also for the drawings in W.B. Tegetmeier's book *Horses, Asses, Zebras, Mules and Mule Breeding*, part of which was also published in serial form in *The Field*. This technique was probably less labour-intensive with the elimination of manual block cutting. It provided softer and more subtle shading, but still allowed the main subject to stand out with strong lines and dark tones.

Halftone printing was not possible until Max Levy, F.E. Ives and others developed the method for process blocks or photo-engraving, making use of photographic techniques and bringing in the potential for printing photographs in books. In the 1890s, process engraving enabled Frohawk to use, firstly, monochrome wash or water-colour drawings such as those in Butler's book on British birds, Frohawk's *Birds Beneficial to Agriculture* and pictures in *The Field* from 1898 and, secondly, the full colour illustrations used in his own butterfly books:

> From the end of 1895 to the end of 1898 I was busy drawing all the plates for British Birds their nests and eggs. The publishers wanted me to supply the whole of the letterpress for the six volumes but I had to decline, as time would not admit of such, having to turn out four plates a week, as well as selecting all the specimens for figuring from the various collections kindly lent by well-known naturalists, also

Drawing of an adder in monochrome water-colour and pencil.

figuring in colour all the eggs of the British Birds, the whole of my time was occupied. When I started this work I was just finishing Scott B. Wilson's important work on the Birds of the Sandwich Islands.

ROUGH AND WORKING DRAWINGS

Frohawk's rough and practice drawings were done in pencil, and by using extremely well-sharpened pencils he was able to prepare some fine and detailed drawings of butterflies and moths for entomological journals. According to his daughter, Frohawk used to sharpen the points of his pencils on a wooden block covered with a fine abrasive paper.

The collection of Frohawk's life's work in the possession of his daughter Valezina and the British Museum (Natural History) is interesting since it includes examples of artwork at all stages of development and also ranging from the beginning of his career in the 1880s up to the very end in the 1940s, a span of over sixty years. There are many very rough sketches, some even done on the backs of old envelopes showing only the roughest outline of a bird, its posture and positioning of wings and legs. These sketches are often heavily annotated with details regarding the colour and nature of plumage and field notes giving locality

Nasua vittata, *a species of coati from South America, painted to illustrate a paper by Lord Rothschild published in his own journal* Novitates Zoologicae, *1909. This water-colour is unsigned, but an almost identical signed version is in the Zoology Library of the British Museum (Natural History).*

Egg of the great auk which measured 13cm in length. This was reproduced as a woodcut in The Field *in 1888 to illustrate an article by Tegetmeier on the sale of this egg at Stevens's Auction Room for the unprecedented sum of £225. The great auk was a flightless bird, once common on Newfoundland, Iceland and the islands off Scotland, but their numbers were depleted, firstly by fishermen and later by collectors until the species became extinct in the mid-nineteenth century.*

and date. Similarly there are many preliminary rough drawings of butterflies, caterpillars and chrysalids.

As well as the rough sketches, there are more detailed working drawings in pencil, sometimes showing a small area of detail like a bill or wing-tip. It has occasionally been possible to find a whole series of pictures of the same animal from the rough field sketch to the finished artwork ready for the publisher. It is surprising how many working drawings there could be leading up to the final copy for publication. In Valezina Bolingbroke's collection there is a fine water-colour of the coati *Nasua vittata*, unsigned but clearly intended for one of Lord Roths-child's papers in the *Novitates Zoologicae*. In the collection at the British Museum (Natural History) there is another identical one that was signed and used. The unsigned one appears to be equally as good and one wonders why it was rejected and another done. Whilst practice is said to make perfect, too much repetition can reduce the spontaneity and spirit of a piece of work. It is interesting that Frohawk's paintings do not seem to show deterioration when they are repeated.

Accuracy is essential when illustrating for scientific publications and Frohawk took such particular care to draw his animals to scale that they received the full approval of the critical Dr Gunther at the British Museum. Frohawk recalls doing some illustrations on reptiles for the *Encyclopaedia Britannica*:

> I recall drawing on wood a tree snake 3 ft. 2 in. long and had to do it on a block of wood 6 in × 3 in on the branch of a tree. This was rather a difficult bit of work as all the intricate scaling had to be done in perspective of each of its twists. On the neck the scales varied much in shape. As an instance how necessary that such drawings should be accurately done, when I showed him the finished drawing, after his critical examination of it he said, 'I do not think you have got that scale (pointing to one on the neck) quite the right shape, but I will refer to the specimen.' He handed back the drawing to me and he only said 'yes you are right' and passed it as correct.

The zoology student is taught to believe and draw what he or she sees because 'the specimen is always right'.

FROHAWK THE NATURALIST

Although Frohawk started his career as an artist, he also came to be recognised as a naturalist, as a specialist in Lepidoptera (butterflies and moths) and as a natural history writer, producing popular articles for *The Field*, particularly when he took over from Tegetmeier as editor of 'The Naturalist' column. In this capacity he was called upon to identify and comment on specimens and queries sent in. The letters column of *The Field*, 'Notes and Queries', which ran for many years was based on these. Having a fairly free hand, Frohawk was able to develop his own ideas into

'Marvellously quick. Study by Mr Frohawk depicting the transitory attitude of a rabbit for the purpose of showing how it happens that the hind foot tracks are impressed on the ground in advance of those of the fore feet.' This pencil drawing was published in The Field *in 1918. One of Frohawk's particular skills was in showing animals in motion and he found this work a special challenge.*

larger feature articles, for which he provided the original observations, the text and illustrations. As well as his connections with *The Field*, Frohawk was on the editorial committee of *The Entomologist*, a journal to which he was also a regular contributor.

Throughout his life, Frohawk kept field notes on natural history which he used from time to time to develop into articles and notes for *The Field*. Some of these notebooks are now with Mr Michael Chalmers-Hunt, who has a particular interest in the history of entomology. Frohawk did not necessarily have to travel far to fill his notebooks; the following observations were made from the window of his study at 'Uplands' in Essex.

During the very severe winter of 1917–18 I noticed rabbits fed largely on the lower foliage of holly, the leaves were all more or less eaten and

Studies of tropical plants painted in water-colour, 1887. In his professional life Frohawk specialised in zoological illustration, but his early oil paintings show an interest in plants and this was also followed in the latter part of his life in Galloway, Scotland, when he had retired from commissioned work. Plants often feature in the backgrounds to his zoological illustrations.

pieces of leaves strewed the snow under the trees. It was in that winter
I worked out and published in *The Field*, drawings of rabbits tracks in
snow, and a drawing of a rabbit running at full speed to show the hind
feet much in advance of the fore feet at each bound. The three species
of shrews occurred. One morning there laid on the front door step a
beautiful pied variety of Water Shrew, killed and brought there by the
cat.

One morning I watched from one of the upper room windows a
stoat and rabbit lopping leisurely along up the meadow, the stoat first
one side of the rabbit then the other and now and again jumping over
it. As they would soon have disappeared through a hedge, I fetched
my gun and fired, the rabbit fell dead and seeing no more of the stoat I
thought it was also killed, but after a few seconds it suddenly
appeared out of a furrow about 70 yds away and scampered down the
meadow in fine style.

After his first butterfly book, *Natural History of British Butterflies*, was published,
more of Frohawk's drawings were produced to accompany his own writing in
book form or as feature articles. In these later years he was not employed only as
an artist or human camera to embellish other people's books, but he was also able
to develop observation, writing and pictures for projects of his own inspiration.
The notes he made in Galloway, just a few years before he died, show his keen
curiosity and enthusiasm for nature was maintained to the end.

Frohawk's life as an artist did not bring much financial reward, but it brought
progressive personal fulfilment. Like another natural history artist, Charles
Tunnicliffe, who followed in his footsteps, Frohawk did not set his sights on
material things.

5

At the Zoo

When Frohawk moved with his family to Croydon, Surrey, in 1873, he was at first reluctant to leave his native East Anglia and spacious country house, and was not too pleased with Croydon. However, there were advantages in being closer to London that played an important part in establishing Frohawk in his chosen career as a naturalist and illustrator. From Croydon and Norwood he had easy access to London – Regent's Park Zoo, the British Museum and, later, meetings of scientific societies. Through these sources Frohawk was able to make many useful contacts in the world of natural history and publishing during the early years of his career.

At the beginning of his teens, in 1874, the young Frohawk made his first visit to the London Zoo at Regent's Park, a place he was to visit regularly for many years

An early pencil sketch of a condor in flight, 1880. It took Frohawk several years to master the techniques of drawing animals in movement.

Pencil sketch of a lion at London Zoo with an inset showing detail. This would have been the basis for a larger drawing or painting.

to study and sketch the animals there. His early working drawings were in pencil, and it took about two years for him to master the problem of drawing animals that were constantly on the move and to represent them in authentic lifelike poses. Frohawk did not have an art school training, so it was largely in these practical sessions at the zoo that he developed the basic skills necessary to a good zoological artist. His patience and meticulous observations of living animals, together with a mastery of the techniques of drawing and painting and a natural aptitude for the work gave him a firm foundation. Frohawk's accuracy also gained him acceptance and a part in the scientific world, where he made original contributions.

Most of the pencil sketches made at the zoo were developed later in the studio, and it is appropriate that Frohawk's very first picture to be sold was a large oil painting (36 × 24 inches) of a pair of lions at the zoo. Frohawk was nineteen when he made this first sale and took a step forward on the road to being a zoological illustrator.

London Zoo was established in 1827, but did not open to the public until 1848 when the admission charge was 6*d.* a head. It was an exciting place, with new developments happening all the time – new houses for exhibiting the animals, constant enlarging of the collections with more novelties and open lectures by eminent zoologists. By the time Frohawk became acquainted with the zoo, it was already a well-established set-up with regular staffing and a ready supply of new animals. Run by a learned body – The Zoological Society of London – the zoo depended on admission charges from visitors for the larger part of its annual income, so publicity regarding the arrival of new animals was important in keeping up the takings at the gate.

THE ZOO AND *THE FIELD*

The weekly gentleman's magazine, *The Field,* had a natural history column in which readers were kept up to date with additions to the menagerie at the zoo; it published reports of meetings of the Society, public lectures and, sometimes, illustrated articles on the more noteworthy new arrivals. The natural history editor of *The Field* at this time was W.B. Tegetmeier, who was in constant contact with developments at the zoo and whose prolific pen provided the more detailed articles on zoo animals. In 1881, when he was twenty, Frohawk became zoological artist to *The Field* and in this capacity he was frequently sent to the zoo to make drawings of animals to accompany articles by Tegetmeier. A letter in the collection of the British Museum (Natural History) written by Tegetmeier in 1894 begins:

Alexandra Grove
North Finchley.

Dec 7th 1894

Dear Frohawk,
Go to the Gardens and draw the young couple of the new Tree Kangaroo. Smith has made a coloured drawing for the Society and I have got a photograph of them in the trees at the Melbourne Gardens which I shall also reproduce very small . . .

Frohawk's particular style of crisp, detailed drawings was ideal for black and white reproduction in magazines and books which did not aspire to costly colour work. In the late nineteenth century the artist played the role of the photographer today, and although more photographs were being taken in the later years of that century and occasionally used in books, publishers still relied largely on artwork for most book and newspaper illustrations. Already Frohawk had achieved a high

Pencil sketch of a toucan, 1884.

standard, for later in the same letter of 1894 we read:

> Bartlett[1] says the Ostrich drawing, which we cannot use this week, is one of the best ostriches he has ever seen. Put that in your pipe and smoke it.

[1]*A.D. Bartlett, Superintendent at the London Zoo (1859–1897).*

The frilled lizard (Chlamydosaurus kingi) at London Zoo. A drawing in crayon on textured coated paper published in The Field *in 1895 to illustrate an article by W.B. Tegetmeier. Found in Australia, this lizard raises its frill in excitement or threat; it is capable of running away at considerable speed on its large hind legs.*

The first illustration by Frohawk to be published in *The Field* was the rubiginous cat in December 1881 and this, like all the early examples up to 1891, was a woodcut. From the dates attached to some drawings, it appears that commissioned works were prepared only a short time before publication. Although called upon to do other natural history illustrations for the magazine, the zoo work formed the bulk of Frohawk's early contributions to *The Field* and they were to provide useful experience which he used at later dates. In the 1890s, Frohawk drew tree kangaroos at the zoo and this work from life helped when he went on to illustrate Lord Rothschild's monograph on these animals published in the *Transactions of the Zoological Society of London* in 1936. Many of these illustrations were reconstructions made from studies of flat preserved skins of tree kangaroos, and in the introduction Lord Rothschild pays tribute to Frohawk's skill. Without the early years of observing living animals at the zoo, he would not have been in such a good position to make artistic reconstructions from unmounted museum specimens.

Commissions for *The Field* led to illustrations of a wide range of animals, from reptiles, such as the frilled lizard, and birds, including various sorts of penguins, to mammals, with browsers such as the zebra and giraffe, carnivores such as the Tasmanian wolf (marsupial) and primates (monkeys, gorillas and gibbons).

THE MONKEY HOUSE

Frohawk spent a good deal of time in the monkey house, especially in the first decade of the twentieth century when he was commissioned to illustrate apes for Lord Rothschild who was then writing about them. The very sensitive drawings of primates suggest that he had a particular regard for these animals, and his zoo work included a splendid series of coloured portraits of chimpanzees looking very lifelike with the highlights of the eyes well painted. Such detailed work involved going into the cage as Frohawk relates.

> The various Apes at the Zoo were always friendly towards me, I suppose showing no fear and treating them quietly and with kindness they seemed very docile. A friendly young Orang about 10 years old that had just been acquired (in 1905) with an expanse of 6 ft 4 in from tip to tip of fingers and great hands and teeth could have pulled my limbs off had it been so disposed. Being anxious to make a careful coloured portrait of his wonderful face, I had at my own risk to enter his big cage so as to be able to examine closely the curiously granulated skin of the face, and other details, also to take measurements of his entire body. I also managed to open wide his great mouth and found he had a well-developed uvula. Upon entering his cage and locking the door, he fortunately received me on friendly terms, after grasping my arm with his great and powerful hand, and even allowed

moloch monkey (*Callithrix moloch*) Brazil. pencil Dec. 12th /82 (F)

The moloch monkey at the zoo. A pencil sketch made in preparation for a woodcut published in The Field, *1882.*

me to sit on the straw beside him, a very satisfactory proceeding, as it enabled me to examine him minutely and take accurate measurements. At the age of twenty-one his whole appearance was greatly altered both as regards the colouring of his face, hair and the remarkable development of the great cheek callosities. Owing to his savage disposition and enormous strength it prevented me taking all his measurements, it will give an idea of his size to note the expanse of his ponderous arms were over 9 ft from tips of his fingers.

The regular appearance of an artist in a cage in the monkey house did not escape notice, and Frohawk's daughter remembers her father relating anecdotes and comments from visitors. On one occasion, two workmen seeing Frohawk in a cage

Monochrome water-colour portrait of a young orang-utan published in The
Field *in 1905. A later article in* The Field *in 1916 reported on the changes
in temperament of this initially docile animal as it became mature.*

were greatly amused, and one commented to the other: 'Which is the ruddy
monkey?'

In 1898 a siamang gibbon was received at Regent's Park, the first example to
be seen in Europe, and in November of the same year a drawing of it by Frohawk
was published in *The Field*.

65

JUMBO THE ELEPHANT

Jumbo the elephant was one of the favourite animals at London Zoo. He was obtained as a young animal of three to four years old in 1865, and the sale of this particular elephant in 1882 attracted a good deal of attention from the public. Jumbo, like all male African elephants, developed dangerous tendencies and only one of the keepers, Matthew Scott, was able to enter the pen. Fearing an accident to a member of the public, the Superintendent, A.D. Bartlett, requested a means of killing Jumbo should the need arise and a rifle was duly obtained. This was never used, however, because the zoo received an offer of £2,000 for the animal from a circus and this was readily accepted. The next problem was that the purchaser, Barnum, was an American and Jumbo had to be crated, conveyed to the dock and put aboard an ocean-going liner for the United States. This was not completed without difficulty, as Frohawk explains:

> Being rather uncertain in temperament it was decided to send him to New York. For this undertaking a huge wooden box-cage was made. After a good deal of suspicion he entered the box but the excessive weight, about 7 tons, caused the trolley to sink into the gravel, this was overcome in the second trial and he was safely shipped to America, but he met his end upon arrival at New York station, where he roamed along the railway, where he came into collision with a train, which caused his death.

Jumbo was duly drawn by Frohawk, and from a pencil working drawing a sepia was prepared.

> Before he left the zoo, I made a sepia drawing of him and exhibited it in the Crystal Palace picture gallery, the same day it was sold after being on exhibition for only one hour.

Jumbo remained an attraction after his death, since his skin was preserved and mounted, and it was in this form that Jumbo returned to England in 1889 with Barnum's Show at Olympia in London, an event reported by Tegetmeier in *The Field*.

The general public have a tendency to take a sentimental attitude towards zoo animals, presenting them with all sorts of highly unsuitable gifts, especially food packages which were regularly received at the zoo office. Frohawk records this:

> The public went almost crazy over this elephant, so much so that all kinds of things arrived daily by post. I remember one day when in the Office a parcel arrived addressed to 'Jumbo', which contained two doz. oysters and a dozen sponge cakes, the former were as unsuitable

Pencil sketch of Jumbo the famous elephant at London Zoo, which may have been the preliminary drawing for a sepia to which Frohawk refers in his memoir. The sale of this elephant was announced in The Field *in 1882. Contrary to Frohawk's recollections, Jumbo had been at London Zoo since 1865 as a young elephant of three to four years old, but as he approached maturity, he became unreliable and, being a safety hazard to the public, was sold in 1882. Another note in* The Field *(January 1883) reported Jumbo escaping from his building by prising off the boards with his tusks. His keeper, Scott, was the only person who could control the elephant; at the Zoo he slept in a room over the elephant house and he went to America with Jumbo when he was sold.*

for an elephant as they were suitable for us in the office. Each morning two nuns visited him to kneel and offer up prayers for his safety. It is astonishing how ignorant the general public are related to anything connected with natural history. The absurd remarks I have heard made by visitors there, were most amusing. I remember a little boy being told by his father (who was quite serious) that he supposed that the lions were clipped about every month. While painting the lions, I often saw the visitors throw into their dens such things as nuts and buns, thinking they would relish them.

Lions, of course, are strictly carnivorous and do not have the omnivorous tendencies of the household dog.

FROHAWK'S RELATIONSHIP WITH ANIMALS

Captive animals can learn to recognise those who regularly spend time with them and the elephant especially is reputed to have a long memory. Further accounts of memory in zoo animals are given in Frohawk's notes.

The recognition of animals to certain persons is well exemplified by the following. When passing a certain wolf, he showed evident pleasure on seeing me, and was quite excited when I stroked and petted him. It was about seven months after I again went in his direction and when at least 50 yds distant he saw me approaching, he became much excited and made so much noise that the keeper came from the back of the dens to see what was the cause of the row as he never heard him making such an ado. It is wonderful the dislike animals take of some people, and the friendly affection to others. It is the same with birds, I was once given a large mussel-crested Cockatoo which was the terror of the household. As soon as I saw it I spoke gently to it and by its general behaviour I felt sure it would be friendly, therefore when I got home with it I opened the cage door and awaited results. The first thing it did was to climb up my arm and perch on my shoulder, speaking softly, instead of savagely attacking me, it caressed me by rubbing its beak on my cheek and from that minute it could not have been more docile and affectionate. To others in the house it showed great hatred and would savagely attack them if it had the chance.

This was not the only pet parrot which Frohawk kept during his lifetime. At one stage he had an Amazon parrot (with green and yellow plumage) and this bird continued to remember him after he gave it to the zoo.

In 1892 I gave an Amazon Parrot to the zoo. I had it before it was fully fledged and kept it for 20 years, it was very affectionate and knew several sentences. I next saw her fully six months after leaving her there. Directly I entered the Parrot House although not in view, she recognised my steps, and when I saw her she was prancing up and down the perch with crown feathers crest like and tail fully expanded shouting out all she knew and when I spoke to her she was in the

68

Monochrome water-colour drawing of Grevy's zebra, published in The
Field *(1899) to illustrate an article by Tegetmeier. This particular animal
was given to the London Zoo by Her Majesty Queen Victoria.*

height of excitement making so much noise that the keeper came up to
see what it was all about. It is a good instance of the retentive memory
possessed by birds.

Frohawk had a way with animals, having pets of his own as well as visiting those
at the zoo, and he happily handled all kinds of improbable pets, one of which was a
snake.

Another interesting pet was a very tame Grass Snake about 2 ft long
which I had for about three years, it became intelligent or I might say
affectionate enough to be caressed and enjoyed to pass the day coiled

Silvery gibbon, monochrome water-colour drawing.

Measurements of the silvery gibbon.

up between the back of my shirt and waistcoat, each morning its basket was placed on a table some distance from the table on which I worked. As soon as I had started it would leave its basket, creep from the table onto mine, over my drawing board and under my waistcoat and snug up on my back all day. On one occasion when I attended a meeting in London, forgetting the snake was up my back, during the meeting it appeared out of the front of my waistcoat and peered round the room, much to the surprise of the members, then quietly retired to its former abode.

Being by birth a countryman, Frohawk was not sentimental over animals but respected them, enjoyed their company and was concerned over their welfare, being aware of the dependence of captive creatures on man for their basic needs. There was a time at the zoo when the lions were on short rations and Frohawk was soon to rise and support their case in print in *The Field*.

In 1891 I protested in *The Field* about the apparently very small amount of food daily supplied to the Lions at the Zoo. Their condition was very much on the thin side, and at feeding time they always appeared ravenous. A wild Lion will be feeding practically all night, every now and again, resting while gorging itself with food. Anyhow after my protestation, the Zoo lions were better fed.

Pencil sketch of a gorilla in its cage at the zoo. Frohawk did many illustrations of primates in the monkey house. A crayon drawing of a gorilla was published in The Field *in 1896.*

Having been closely associated with the zoo since the beginning of his commissioned work for *The Field* in 1881 and having a great liking for animals, in the autumn of 1898 Frohawk joined forces with the Earl of Llandaff with the intention (with the aid of Lord Rothschild) of acquiring a property to run as a zoological garden. They settled on the fine mansion and spacious gardens of Duddles Villa in Kemptown overlooking Brighton, but the scheme fell through in March 1899 'owing to those responsible for the prospectuses not being ready on the day advertised. I was a ruined man in consequence.' No further details are given on this venture, but from his last remark it is evident that Frohawk must have invested most of his capital in this, which was then lost. In addition, the Brighton zoo project took up considerable time during which he was not available for commissioned work to bring in an income. Following the collapse, he went to stay in Staffordshire and launched himself back into his artwork. All this happened within three years of Frohawk's first marriage, when he had a wife and two infants to support.

CRYSTAL PALACE

As well as the London Zoo, animals were also available for study at the Crystal Palace, near Croydon. There were many exhibitions there – zoo animals, an aquarium and a fine museum of mounted animals (the Wartenburg Collection), together with displays of butterflies and moths. There was also a picture gallery where Frohawk hung and sold some of his early works. Crystal Palace was another place of inspiration and in particular there is mention of the monkey house 'where I spent several days sketching them and various other animals'.

Important shows of dogs, cats, pigeons and poultry were held at Crystal Palace and attended by Frohawk in various capacities: as an exhibitor – when his large, long-haired tabby tom cat was awarded first prize in 1889 – and as an artist sketching many of the show animals for practice, commissions and publication. The atmosphere, however, was to change:

> Since the commercial exhibitions were opened in the end of the 80's, the Palace began to lose its dignity, until then it was one of the most silent places of entertainment. A season ticket available for a year was only £1.

The original Crystal Palace building, erected during 1852–54 with materials from the great Hyde Park Exhibition of 1851, lasted until 1937 when:

> This wonderful building containing works of high art and treasures of priceless value, was with the exception of the great towers destroyed by the disastrous fire 1937. One of the Nation's greatest losses. In April 1941 the north tower was blown up with 220 lbs of gelatine dynamite. The scrap from the tower weighed 840 tons, which was consigned to the melting pot for war munitions.

6

Illustrating The Field

Illustrations for 'The Naturalist' column of *The Field* provided the young Frohawk with his first regular artwork on commission. He had met the previous zoological illustrator, T.W. Wood, at the British Museum and it was through him that Frohawk came to illustrate for *The Field*. This important step in his early career is best explained in his own words.

> Early in 1881, I called at *The Field* office, then in The Strand, to announce to the Editor, the death of T.W. Wood, who had been Zoological Artist to the paper. He had expressed a wish that in the event of his failing health, I should replace him in that capacity. I was therefore introduced by the Editor-in-Chief Mr. Walsh to W.B. Tegetmeier then acting as Natural History Editor. He at once commissioned me to draw the fresh arrival at the Zoo. Gdns. The Rubiginous Cat an Indian species, which was published in *The Field* 1881, my first published drawing (a woodcut). Since that date a great many of my drawings of various mammals, birds, reptiles, fishes and insects have appeared in its columns. These were accompanied by his [Tegetmeier's] articles until a few years before he passed away in 1912 at the age of 96.

Illustrating for *The Field* started in a small way, with one or two drawings commissioned each year up to 1885; this then increased to three or four and later rose to as many as eight in a year (1895). This formed a substantial part of Frohawk's livelihood in the early years of his career, and also led to other commissions from the editorial staff of *The Field* who were writing books and articles.

Looking through Frohawk's artwork in *The Field* from 1881 onwards, we can see an interesting transition in the medium which he used. The earliest pictures were woodcuts, a common though laborious method of illustration at the time; while Frohawk made the drawing on wood, the block itself was cut by someone else. In these early woodcuts Frohawk's distinctive signature is usually shown in the bottom left-hand corner, whilst that of the block cutter appears in the right-hand corner. Frohawk's illustrations in *The Field* took the form of woodcuts from 1881 until 1890 and the block cutter throughout was C. Butterworth. These illustrations provided sharp and crisp images.

As was described in Chapter 4, the woodcut technique of illustration was

*The rubiginous cat (*Felis rubiginosa) *from Sri Lanka (Ceylon). This woodcut was Frohawk's first commissioned drawing for* The Field *and was published in 1881 to illustrate an article by W.B. Tegetmeier on this new arrival at London Zoo. The woodcut is signed by both the artist and the block cutter.*

superseded in 1891 in Frohawk's work for *The Field* by drawings in crayon on coated textured paper. By 1898 the crayon drawings had given way to another technique, that of monochrome water-colour drawings, and this became the hallmark of Frohawk's later style of illustration used for books, journals and magazines. These monochrome water-colour or wash drawings were executed in fine detail, with the main subject in strong punchy tone against a more impressionistic but still accurate background showing the habitat. This style lent itself very well to bird illustration, with the birds shown in relation to the places in which they were found.

Frohawk illustrated a wide range of zoological subjects. Since *The Field* kept its readers in touch with new arrivals at London Zoo Frohawk often drew foreign animals in captivity, but he also prepared illustrations of the native British fauna to accompany articles on natural history or showing specimens sent to the editor.

The goliath beetle (Goliathus goliatus = G. druryi), *a drawing in crayon on textured coated paper to illustrate an article by W.B. Tegetmeier in* The Field, *1893. This beetle was drawn at the zoo.*

Abnormal head of a kudu. Crayon on textured coated paper to illustrate an article by W.B. Tegetmeier in The Field, *1893. There was considerable interest in abnormal specimens of animals, which were frequently reported in* The Field. *This one was exhibited at a meeting of the Zoological Society of London by Mr F.C. Selous, a distinguished naturalist on Africa.*

W.B. TEGETMEIER

Frohawk worked closely with *The Field*'s natural history editor, W.B. Tegetmeier, a man some forty-five years his senior, from whom he gained much useful experience of the world of natural history and also a training in journalism and publishing. He describes Tegetmeier in his memoir:

> He was in many respects outstanding in knowledge and experience with a wide circle of admirers . . . He was an authority on Poultry, Pigeons and other domestic creatures, and published works concerning them. His opinions were sought by Darwin.

It was through Tegetmeier that Frohawk met Charles Darwin himself.

> Charles Darwin I once met at *The Field* office in 1881, when he called to see W.B. Tegetmeier about poultry. I was introduced to him. How interested he would have been, had I then discovered the wonderful association between the Large Blue Butterfly larvae and Ants.

At the time of this meeting, Frohawk would have been twenty years of age and Darwin sixty-two.

W.B. Tegetmeier had the reputation of a great character, and was closely associated with the magazine from the time of the publication of his first article in 1859 until he retired from editorial duties in 1907 at the advanced age of ninety-one. Tegetmeier is generally remembered for his book on the rearing of pheasants, *Pheasants for Coverts and Aviaries: their Natural History and Practical Management*, but he was also a great expert on pigeons, bee-keeping and poultry. His earlier training in the practice of medicine had provided Tegetmeier with the scientific skills of dissection and investigation of disease. He also had an interest in art (he used to collect etchings) and he initiated an annual report in *The Field* on 'Natural History at the Royal Academy', in which task he was later joined by Frohawk. Some works impressed them more than others as Frohawk explains:

> Some of these were absurdities and were treated in the comments as they deserved.

The Savage Club, formed in the 1850s by a group of authors, journalists and artists, revered Tegetmeier as one of their founder members.

> His portrait hangs in the Savage Club of which he was one of the original members and where I frequently dined with him. Having lived all his long life in London his knowledge of it and its environs were encyclopaedic . . . Before the days of matches, he saw people

W.B. Tegetmeier (1816–1912), natural history editor to The Field, *who helped Frohawk develop a career in zoological illustration and writing. Frohawk eventually replaced him as natural history editor.*

standing by their open doors early in the morning holding lighted rush-lights for their neighbours to borrow a light . . . In the early nineties he told me what constituted the greatest change in London was the enormous number of people in the streets. When a young man in such places as the Strand only a comparatively few pedestrians would be seen.

Compare this with The Strand in the rush hour today!

Young king vulture. Drawing in crayon on textured coated paper published in The Field, *1893. This young bird proved tame and playful when confined in a room with the artist, sitting on Frohawk's feet, tugging at his trousers and snatching his pencil.*

Monochrome water-colour drawing of a siamang, one of the gibbons, that was published in The Field, *1896. This was a new arrival at London Zoo and it was the first time that a siamang had been on show in Europe. W.B. Tegetmeier reported on the great difficulty in keeping anthropoid apes alive for any length of time in Britain's uncongenial climate, and he recommended readers to see this animal immediately.*

Tegetmeier trained initially as a surgeon and practised medicine until he was twenty-five, when his father died. He then gave up the financial security of a medical career for the insecure and less profitable world of writing, augmented initially by lecturing. From this change of lifestyle and value judgement he considered himself a Bohemian.

Although over forty-five years apart in age, Frohawk and Tegetmeier had much in common in their outlook on life. Both were born in the country but had to learn to adapt to life in built-up areas at the beginning of their teens. With less scope for the study of natural history in their new urban locations, Frohawk and Tegetmeier both took an interest in domesticated and captive animals and in the world of showing. Neither of them followed the future that their respective families had envisaged for them. As a result of ten years in medicine Tegetmeier had a scientific training which Frohawk did not have, but in their work as colleagues on *The Field* Tegetmeier was primarily a writer and Frohawk an artist first and writer later. In spite of their reluctance to leave the countryside of their childhood, both men

Poitou mule brunette. Drawing in crayon on textured coated paper to illustrate the book Horses, Asses, Zebras, Mules and Mule Breeding *by W.B. Tegetmeier and C.L. Sutherland (1895). Many of the illustrations for this book were also published in* The Field.

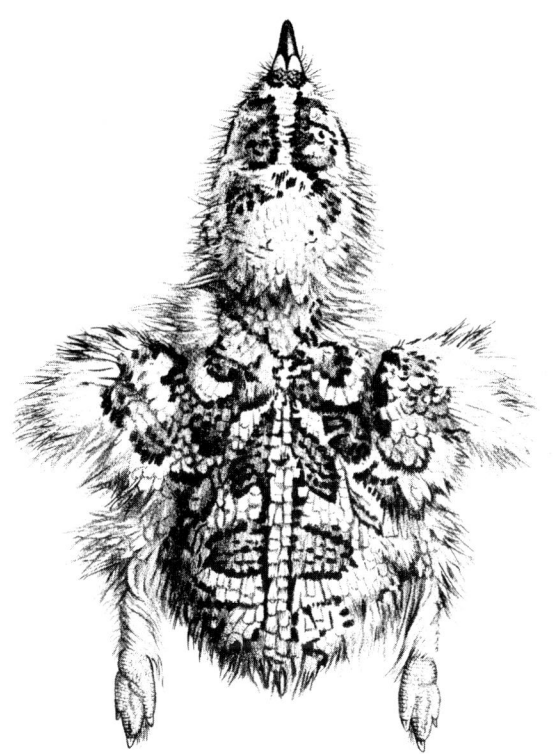

Monochrome water-colour drawing of the chick of Pallas's sand grouse. This dead chick was sent to Professor Newton of Cambridge, who immediately asked Frohawk to make a coloured drawing for The Ibis. *It was also redrawn on wood for* The Field, *1890.*

stayed in the London area for the rest of their days. In their private lives they married at a similar age, Tegetmeier was twenty-nine and Frohawk was thirty-three, and they both had a long association with *The Field*, Tegetmeier from 1859 until 1907 and Frohawk from 1881 until 1945. Frohawk did many illustrations for Tegetmeier's numerous articles in *The Field*, some of which were also used in his books, including *Horses, Asses, Zebras, Mules and Mule Breeding* (1895). Frohawk also illustrated one of the later editions of a book on dogs written by the chief editor of *The Field*, J.H. Walsh, writing under the pseudonym 'Stonehenge' – it was entitled *The Dogs of Britain, America and other Countries*. Frohawk recollects some of the other editors with whom he worked at *The Field*:

> In the 'eighties' *The Field* was under the Editorship of Mr. Walsh, an authority on shooting and other sports. His well known book 'Stonehenge' on dogs, the last edition published in the eighties, he commissioned me to illustrate. On his death the Editorship passed to Mr. Toms, then in turn to Mr. Senior, Sir Theodore Cook and Mr. Eric Parker. All five Editors whom I intimately knew, and I am pleased to say appreciated my work.

FROHAWK'S EDITORIAL WORK

In 1882 Frohawk made his first written contribution to *The Field*. This was an article on the late stay of swallows and martins, and was followed in 1886 by a note on snipe in a London suburb; both appeared under the 'Notes and Queries' section of 'The Naturalist' column. These were followed in 1887 with entries on clothes moth larvae, pellets ejected by birds and on the previous entomological season. Over the years he was to provide many more contributions for 'Notes and Queries', usually on birds or butterflies but occasionally on other subjects too.

   Frohawk's expert knowledge of Lepidoptera was recognised in his later appointment as entomological editor, assisting Tegetmeier, and this work he recalls in his notes:

Monochrome water-colour drawing of the 'V.C.' pigeon published in The Field, *1918. This bird was awarded a V.C. for its part in the First World War. It was dispatched from the front line with a message, was struck and wounded by an enemy bullet, but reached its destination with the message intact, dying shortly afterwards.*

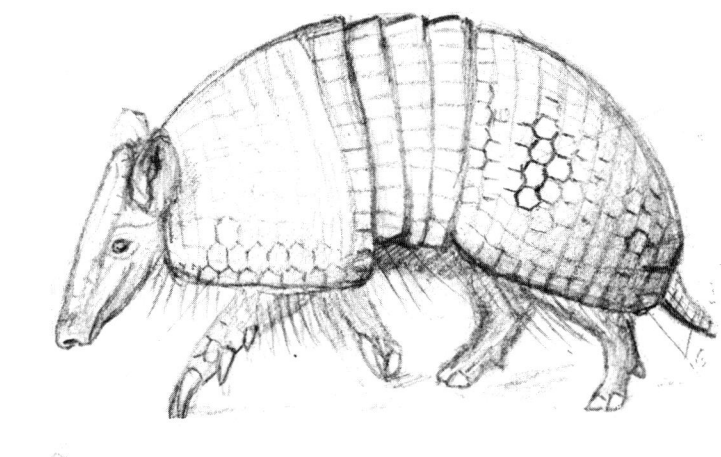

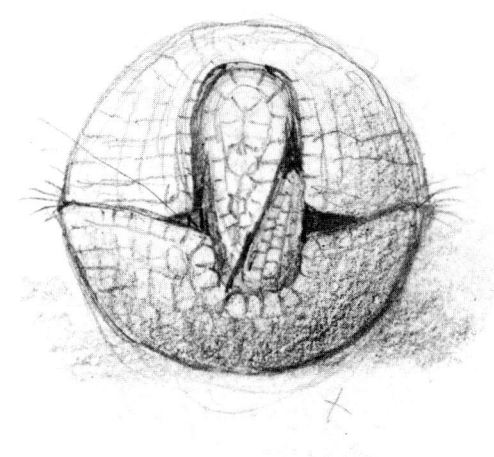

Pencil sketches of the three-banded armadillo (Tolypeutes tricinctus) *that were preliminary to a drawing in crayon on textured coated paper published in* The Field, *1895. London Zoo had acquired a specimen of this animal. Whilst it can roll into a ball like a woodlouse when threatened, this one spent its time running around the room in which it was confined and scatching its ears against the artist's ankles as he sat drawing.*

> Acting as Entomological Editor for the past half century, I received
> many hundreds of enquiries and specimens for identification from
> correspondents, all of which I answered without a failure. Also all
> books relating to the subject were passed on to me for review. During
> the [first] war the Editor, Sir Theodore Cook, in 1915 asked me to
> contribute a series of illustrated articles of the life histories of all our
> British Butterflies. These were published from week to week through-
> out the year. The Editor's idea was to let his readers have something
> to occupy their mind in contrast to war news.

As Tegetmeier approached his last years as editor of 'The Naturalist' column his
drive diminished and he produced less copy. When Frohawk took over as natural
history editor in 1907, the space devoted to natural history was increased; he had
many contributors writing for him and produced a lively section of 'Notes and
Queries'. In the issues in the years preceding World War I, some two-and-a-half
sides were devoted to 'The Naturalist' column. Whilst Frohawk continued to
provide some artwork, many photographs were now being used.

For nearly forty years Frohawk had a happy working relationship with the
editorial staff at *The Field*, people who shared his own values in life. However, this
state of affairs was to change.

> In the 'twenties' *The Field* changed Proprietorship, the staff then
> changed also, the elder men of experience were replaced by younger
> men whose knowledge suffered somewhat from inexperience.

Until the 1930s *The Field* had been a newspaper, but at this point it was redesigned
to become a magazine, and 'The Naturalist' and other regular columns were
discontinued in favour of longer feature articles. The 'Notes and Queries' were
also lost, and any letters from readers were printed together on a general page of
letters to the editor. Frohawk was nearing his seventies when this change came
about, and although after 1930 he contributed less to *The Field* he continued to
submit articles ranging from short notes and queries to longer feature articles, and
this continued right up to his death in 1946, which finally ended an association of
over sixty years.

7

With the Museum

The British Museum (Natural History), together with his connections with *The Field*, played an important part in Frohawk's early career as it provided a source of commissioned artwork and professional contacts for the rest of his life. He first went there as a young man to study specimens behind the scenes in the days when the natural history collections were still at Bloomsbury, before the move to the present site in South Kensington. Frohawk therefore saw the development of the natural history museum we know today and he was, over the years, involved in many aspects of the work that went on there. In his memoir he explains how he came to make contact with the British Museum staff when he was only eighteen:

> In 1879, while studying the plumage of Birds by sketching the expanded wings, the late T.W. Wood, an experienced artist and naturalist whose work I had always admired, made himself known to me, and making very complimentary remarks on my work, resulting in subsequently becoming great friends, both pursuing identical studies.
>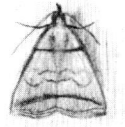
>
> Two years after, in 1881, all the Natural History department was moved to the great Natural History Museum at South Kensington, the then completed building for the reception of the overflowing collection at the old museum at Bloomsbury. It was at the new building I saw the late Dr. A.G. Butler, the then Keeper of Entomology, and showed him a drawing on wood of a Red Admiral on a thistle, which he considered so accurate that he introduced me to Dr. A. Gunther, the Director [*sic*], he being the great authority on Fishes and Reptiles and at once commissioned me to illustrate the catalogue of Fishes. This led me to become an intimate friend of Dr. G. Boulenger, who commissioned me to make a lithographic plate for the Proceedings of the Zoo – this being my second attempt at lithography. From that day I continued drawing various zoological subjects for Museum publications, and other scientific works.

Illustrations for the museum covered a wide field, including fishes, reptiles, mammals and particularly birds, butterflies and moths. Dr Butler, as head of the Entomology Department, was a prolific author, writing papers on Lepidoptera at work and also books on birds in his spare time, and he therefore commissioned many drawings and paintings including colour plates for his paper *Illustrations of typical specimens of Lepidoptera, Heterocera in the collections at the British Museum.*

   Another staff member with whom Frohawk had associated was Dr A.C.L.G. Gunther, who was Keeper or head of the Department of Zoology. Frohawk was introduced to him by Dr Butler and came to know him well:

> Dr. Albert Gunther who was an intimate friend. We had many interesting chats in his private room at the British Museum . . . He was the authority on fish and reptiles. He commissioned me to illustrate the catalogue of fishes and reptiles (wood engravings) for the *Encyclopaedia Britannica* (this was in the end of the 80's before the invention of wash drawings for process blocks).

It seems that Gunther had considerable power over members of his staff, as Frohawk relates:

> He had a great personality and administrative power, it used to amuse me how all the assistants in the Entomological Dept suddenly so seriously assumed their busiest behaviour when he appeared on the scene and would give me a smile as I sat at Dr. A.G. Butler's table figuring insects for him. Although Butler was then Keeper of En-

*Woodcut print showing a poisonous coral snake (*Micrurus fulvius =
Elaps fulvius*) swallowing a non-poisonous snake (*Tantilla
semicinctum = Homalocranium semicinctum*) which illustrated an
entry by Dr Gunther in the* Encyclopaedia Britannica.

tomology, he abandoned at once all levity, and when Gunther used to whistle down the tube from the Director's room to Butler's room in the basement, it was amusing to see Butler drop whatever he was working at and run across the room to the tube in answer to the whistle, being so afraid of keeping Gunther waiting. Telephones were not in use for such purposes in those days.

CONTACTS THROUGH THE MUSEUM

Many interesting people and active biologists in the centre of the research world pass through as visitors to the departments behind the scenes in the Natural History Museum, and Frohawk enjoyed some stimulating meetings:

> At the museum I met many distinguished men of science from various parts, working their specialized groups of the various orders of nature and learned a good deal respecting comparatively little known parts of the world.

From the field of polar research he met the Norwegian explorer Dr Nansen, owner of the *Fram*, the vessel later used by the Norwegian explorer Amundsen when he successfully beat Captain Scott's party in the race to the South Pole:

> I met Dr. Nansen at the British Museum 1893 just before he left on his Polar exploration. We talked upon the Fauna of the Arctic and other subjects of the Far North, also the structure of the *Fram* which had been strengthened to resist the ice pressure.

Other polar explorers Frohawk met included Sir J.G. Jackson of the Jackson Harmsworth Expedition of the 1890s, which undertook zoological research in the Arctic. It was on this expedition that polar bear meat was discovered as a cure for scurvy. In the later ill-fated British Antarctic Expedition of 1910–12, Captain Scott did not seem to be aware of the value of fresh meat as a vitamin source to prevent scurvy. Frohawk contributed to the appendix of Jackson's book, *A Thousand Days in the Arctic*.

In 1904 Frohawk met Captain Scott's right-hand man, Dr. E.A. Wilson on his return from the Discovery Expedition to the Antarctic:

> He told me some of his exploits in those desolate regions. He said only those who have been there have any idea of the dreariness and depressing effect of the gloom of those regions.

Dr Wilson was particularly interested in the embryology of penguin eggs and

*Lithographic print illustrating the moor frog (*Rana arvalis*) to accompany an article by Dr Boulenger in the* Proceedings of the Zoological Society of London. *This was hand coloured in the journal.*

made many studies on these birds:

> The penguins lay their single egg on the snow and work it up to rest on the feet and lower the skin of the belly so as to form a hood covering it to keep it warm for hatching. They breed in colonies and hatch one another's egg being indifferent if it is their own or not. All the young (chicks) he dissected had stones in their stomachs. Obviously directly they are hatched the parents enter the water under the ice to collect the stones to give them to their young to aid digestion of their first meal . . . Wilson was a keen observer of ornithology and skillful artist.

Dr Wilson perished with Scott and Bowers in their tent, just eleven miles from One Ton Depot on the last lap of their return journey from the South Pole, where they discovered that Amundsen's party had arrived first. During the polar winter before this epic journey, Dr Wilson, 'Birdy' Bowers and Apsley Cherry Garrard made an expedition to collect eggs of the emperor penguin for later study. Dr Wilson never lived to do this research, but the only survivor of the three felt duty-bound to deliver the eggs to the British Museum (Natural History). The story of a less than enthusiastic reception is told by Cherry Garrard in his book *The*

Worst Journey in the World, first published in 1922. These famous penguin eggs were blown at the museum by Frohawk.

It is likely that Frohawk and Dr Wilson had a good deal in common, for both were deeply interested in birds, were fine artists and of a quiet disposition. They also met at some of Lord Rothschild's dinners held at his museum of Tring; one of Frohawk's menu-cards bears the signature of E.A. Wilson.

Lord Walsingham was another contact made through the museum and his particular interest was moths.

> In many respects Lord Walsingham was outstanding in sport and scientific research. He contributed largely to our knowledge of entomology. I had the pleasure of his friendship for many years and found him a most able field naturalist and scientific observer. In 1888 he commissioned me to illustrate his monograph on the micros (small moths) he collected in Canada numbering about 1000 specimens. Also his work on the African Tigeneria a wonderful and beautiful family of very small moths. It was that year I lunched with him at Walsingham House, Piccadilly (now the Ritz Hotel) when he had just had Electric Light installed in all the main rooms, a novelty to me then. He was also fascinated by the switching on and off of the lights . . . I met him at the British Museum the next day after his great grouse shoot on his Bloober House Moors, Yorkshire when he made the record bag . . . After all his wealthy life of sport and pleasures, he passed away in comparative poverty.

In his museum contacts, Frohawk was surrounded by those who had travelled the world in search of natural history and whose stories he was eager to hear. On one occasion he had a chance to join two expeditions to distant countries:

> It was at the museum early in 1895 I met the Maragh Dulap Sing and Lord Walsingham, they wanted me to go as naturalist for a years exploration round the world on his yacht, calling at remote tropical islands and other little worked islands collecting natural history specimens, and gave me a fortnight to decide. Of course it would have been a great experience and a chance of a lifetime and things of great consequence often clash. It was only 3 weeks after two friends asked me to accompany them as naturalist on a trip of 3,000 miles up the Amazon. But having just made arrangements for my marriage that spring it would have been dis-loyal and a selfish act on my part to accept these outstanding opportunities, and I was compelled to refuse.

WORK FOR THE MUSEUM

Throughout his long life Frohawk spent many hours making illustrations for staff at the museum, and from the use of preserved specimens he built up an extensive knowledge of the structure and detail of animals. Not all the material he worked from had been mounted by taxidermists, very large numbers of research specimens are stored as flat skins, and from these he was expected to make three dimensional lifelike illustrations. Here Frohawk's time spent studying and drawing animals from life at London Zoo proved invaluable, for he was not only able to reproduce correctly the overall shape, but also to give the animal its natural characteristic posture – something which only comes from first-hand experience.

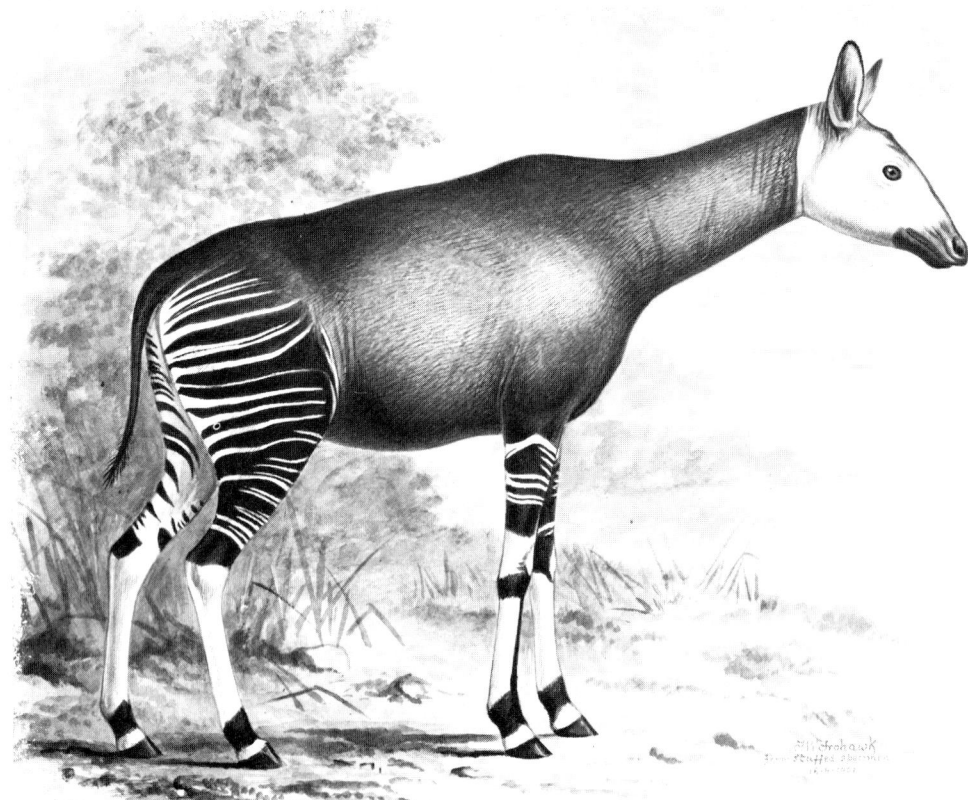

*Okapi (*Okapia johnstonii*) drawn from a mounted specimen in the British Museum (Natural History). Monochrome water-colour and pencil drawing published in* The Field *in 1901. The okapi had only recently been discovered in Africa and the skin was presented to Sir Harry Johnston after whom the species was named. It was set up and mounted by the famous taxidermist Rowland Ward of Piccadilly and was on public display in the Museum.*

Frohawk's work at the museum had been largely as a zoological artist, but the director asked him to write as well as illustrate a book, *Birds Beneficial to Agriculture*, that was published by the museum in 1919 and linked to an exhibition. This involved securing specimens for mounting by the well-known taxidermist and natural history dealer Rowland Ward of Piccadilly. The exhibition was set up in the central hall of the museum. The original monochrome water-colour illustrations for this book are now in the Zoology Library of the British Museum (Natural History).

Another museum project he was commissioned to do was a series of coloured postcards showing the life cycles of butterflies and moths in April 1928. These were also sold in book form with an appended text, and both were for sale at the museum until the late 1950s. The original water-colour paintings are in the Entomology Library of the museum and the richness in the colour of these show that the printings did not do the work justice.

Being a freelance artist and not a permanent member of the staff of the museum,

Hartlaub's duck. Monochrome water-colour drawn from a skin in the collections of the British Museum (Natural History).

Frohawk does not feature in William T. Stearn's book *The Natural History Museum at South Kensington* (1981). Nevertheless, he was part of the hum of museum activity, working regularly in various departments, and it is appropriate that the museum holds a good collection of original work by Frohawk in the Zoology Library and in the Department of Entomology. Lord Rothschild bought one of his insect collections, so in fact some of Frohawk's specimens are within the Rothschild Collection at the museum.

It was through the museum that Frohawk came to meet the Hon. Walter Rothschild, later Lord Rothschild. Lord Rothschild built and ran his own museum at Tring in Hertfordshire, where he amassed a most impressive zoological collection that, on his death, was bequeathed to the nation and is now run as an outstation of the British Museum (Natural History). Frohawk described his first meeting with Walter Rothschild:

> The late Lord Rothschild (then the Hon. Walter Rothschild) came into the insect department (in 1889) and admired my work so much that he asked me to do a coloured plate for the Zoo Proceedings to accompany his paper on some fine new species of moths from the Solomon Is. From then until his death in August 1937, I had the continuous pleasure of making for him drawings and paintings of Mammals, Birds, Reptiles, Fishes and Insects. His important work on *Extinct Birds* published at £25, with a large number of coloured plates. Some of these I did including the Dodo's and the gigantic Moa (*Dinornis ingens*): this was reproduced for the book. I did this huge bird

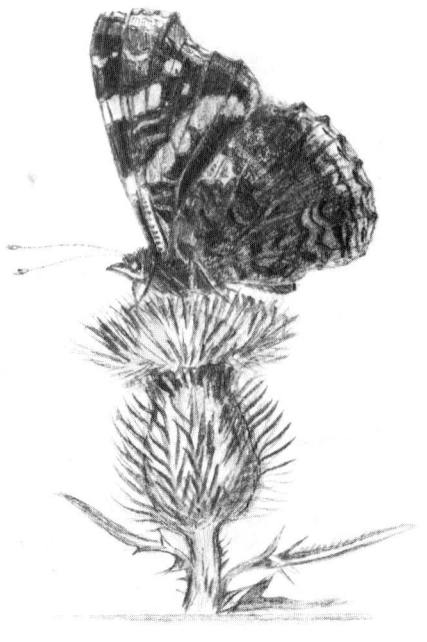

Preliminary drawing of a red admiral on a thistle intended for use as a wood engraving, but the marked block was never cut. It was probably this drawing that was referred to in Frohawk's memoir when Dr Butler introduced him to Dr Gunther of the British Museum who commissioned drawings for his publications.

from the skeleton (in the British Museum) which is 11 ft 6 ins. in height from the crown of the skull to the soles of the toes and restored the entire bird from feathers found preserved in a cave in New Zealand.

Further descriptions of the moa painting are given in Chapter 9.

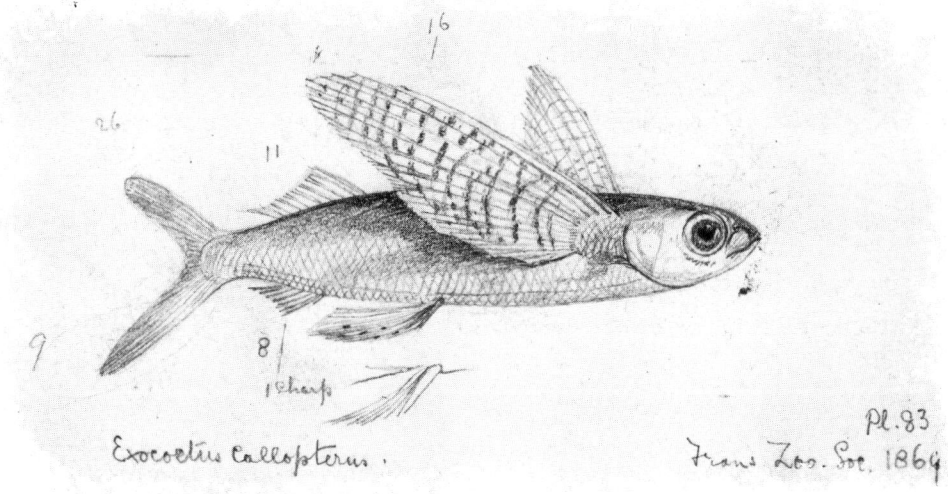

Flying fish (Exocoetus callopterus); *the enlarged pectoral fins act as parachutes, enabling the fish to glide above water.*

Lord Rothschild was a regular visitor to the museum, serving there as one of its trustees. Although quite different personalities (Lord Rothschild was distinctly eccentric), they were in many ways kindred spirits, sharing their strong interest in natural history. Both men, of similar age, had a privileged childhood, both became keen on natural history at an early age, and for both natural history was the central pivot of their lives. Walter Rothschild, following dismissal from his part in the family banking business, worked very long hours in his museum and appreciated high standards in everything. He took immediately to Frohawk's accurate and attractive illustrations. Walter Rothschild was of a retiring nature, he had great personal difficulties and in public he was hampered by a stammer. He was happier and more confident in his museum and in the company of naturalists than anywhere else. Lord Rothschild sometimes visited Frohawk at his home at Sutton, Surrey, and he frequently asked him to come and visit and help in his museum at Tring. Frohawk also came to know his brother the Hon. Charles Rothschild, another keen naturalist and entomologist and an expert on fleas – work which he carried on alongside his traditional family career in finance.

8

The Entomological World

As we have already seen, Frohawk was fascinated by insects from very early childhood taking a special interest in butterflies and moths. At the age of five he had his own copy of W.S. Coleman's *British Butterflies* (1860), not an easy book for a young child to use. His parents encouraged the study of natural history, and as he was brought up in the country there was every opportunity to develop the hobby. Frohawk's early butterfly collecting was mostly done alone, although in a note in *The Field* (26 November 1887) he mentions collecting with his brother. He did not, however, come to know any entomologists until later in life and his early artwork was largely confined to country landscapes and mammals, birds, reptiles, amphibians and fish.

Frohawk's first step into the entomological world was his meeting in 1881 with Dr A.G. Butler, Keeper of Entomology at the British Museum (Natural History), and through him came the first commissioned work illustrating Lepidoptera. Over the years, Frohawk provided drawings and paintings for many of Dr Butler's papers and also for those of Lord Rothschild and Lord Walsingham; all these people were prolific authors.

THE SOUTH LONDON ENTOMOLOGICAL
AND NATURAL HISTORY SOCIETY

In 1886 Frohawk joined the South London Entomological and Natural History Society[1] which was just recovering from a low ebb when its membership dropped to around forty. We can follow much of his involvement with the Society from the *Proceedings*, published annually, which reported fully on the exhibitions and discussions at meetings. In 1886, Frohawk's talents were called upon to provide a frontispiece plate, something which continued for the next two years. He attended a meeting on 21 January 1886 and exhibited an ichneumon fly bred from a beetle. At that time the South London Entomological and Natural History Society held

[1] *Now known as The British Entomological and Natural History Society.*

96

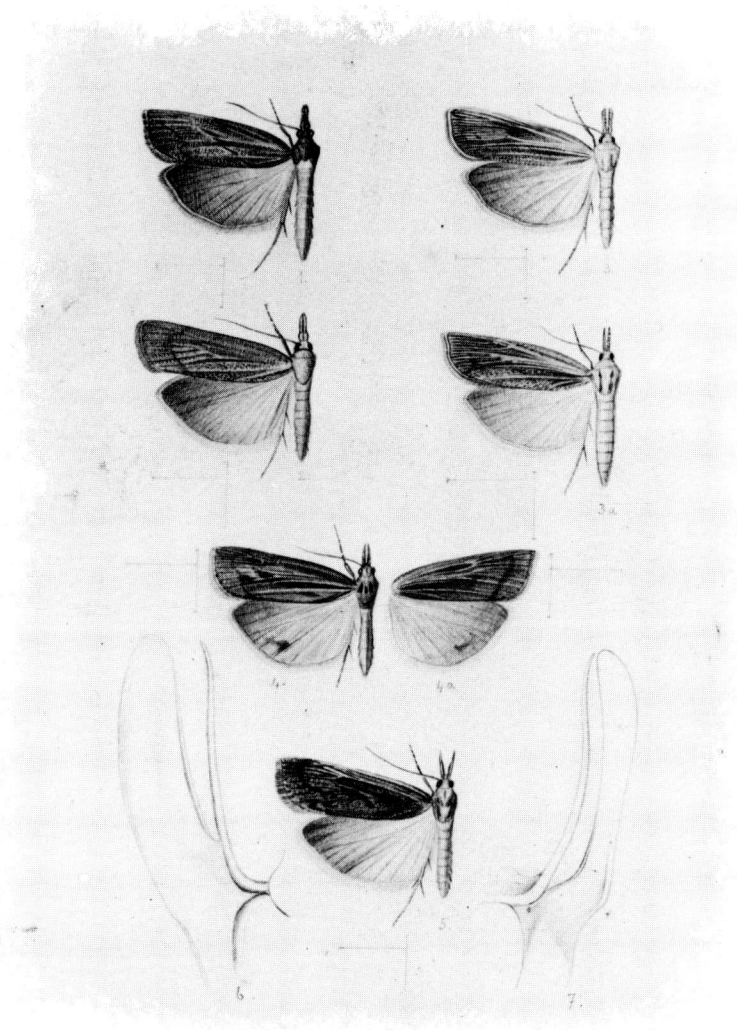

Moths. A plate for reproduction as a coloured lithograph in a scientific journal.

two meetings a month in London, which centred around exhibits brought by members, the reading of occasional papers and discussion arising. The indoor meetings were attended by about thirty members and there appears, from the reports, to have been a hard core of regular attenders, of whom Frohawk was one, who could be relied upon to bring exhibits. Field meetings were arranged on Saturday afternoons to the countryside around London, but these were not so well

Frohawk and Captain Douglas Forsyth Johnstone in the field with their butterfly nets. Hadleigh Woods, Essex, May 1921.

supported and, although reported in the *Proceedings*, there is no record (with a few exceptions) of who attended them.

Frohawk was an active member of the Society and in 1892, when he was elected to serve on the council, he attended as many as eleven meetings. He took his responsibilities as a council member seriously and was a regular attender at meetings over the next few years. The Society had recovered from its earlier doldrums and in 1894 boasted a membership of 189, when better support for the field meetings was also reported.

At this time, two prominent members who served on the council were Richard South and J.W. Tutt, both active workers on Lepidoptera. Other members included John Carrington, who wrote on insects for *The Field*, Robert Adkin, a loyal supporter of the Society and later President, and the popular natural history writer Edward Step of the 'Wayside and Woodland Series' published by Warne. Members of the Society were primarily amateur collectors who took an avid interest in specimens showing any varietal differences that might be added to their cabinets.

*Pencil drawing of the small heath (*Coenonympha pamphilus). *This ubiquitous species is on the wing from mid-May until October and in England there are two broods during the season. It overwinters as a caterpillar.*

There was a strong tradition in the Society for breeding butterflies from eggs or caterpillars, and this had the attraction of producing pristine specimens for collections. The rich colours of freshly emerged butterflies fade when they have been subjected to the sun and weather for a few days and the wings may also get damaged. Frohawk did a lot of butterfly rearing; sometimes he would put a female he had caught on an appropriate plant to lay eggs in captivity and these would be reared to maturity. All of this was very time-consuming but the effort was rewarded by the interesting variants that occasionally turned up. Many of Frohawk's exhibits at meetings consisted of juvenile stages or adult butterflies reared in captivity, but sometimes, as on 8 March 1894, he commented on other

*Pencil drawing of the caterpillar of the pale clouded yellow (*Colias hyale), *a butterfly native to the Mediterranean which occasionally migrates to the British Isles.*

aspects of natural history such as the presence of both stoat and weasel on Tooting Common.

H.J. Turner, reporting on the field meeting to Wisley on 7 July 1894, suggested there was a happy atmosphere in the Society when he wrote:

> This may not have been a very brilliant meeting looked at from the point of view of one avaricious for specimens, but I think that, like most of our excursions, it will be looked back upon as one of those days in our lives when we learnt a great deal of Nature's method, and when we were supremely happy in the close communion of those of like tastes with ourselves, obtaining the relaxation from various business cares, and seeing, by means of the glasses, as it were, of biological knowledge, much more in the world around us than the majority of those we jostled against by the way.

There is no evidence, however, that Frohawk attended field meetings; he was probably too busy with commissioned work and publishers' deadline dates to give up a Saturday afternoon.

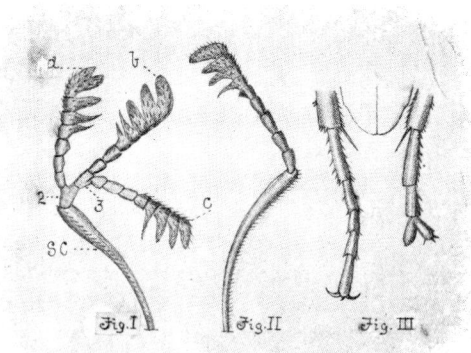

A pencil drawing of beetle legs to illustrate a paper by Garbowski in The Entomologist, *1895.*

As with many societies, most of the work was carried out by a small proportion of the membership, and in the President's Address of 1895 it was suggested that things were 'too much confined to a few willing friends'. Frohawk served on the council again in 1896, but only for a year. From Richard South's Presidential Address of 1896, we have hints of some uncomfortable personal undercurrents at the meetings, such that South felt a few words were necessary:

> We should remember that it is not by mere verbosity and liberal use of the first person singular that we are most likely to convince others of our being right, and their being wrong . . . Difference of opinion leads to discussion but the legitimate outcome of argument should be elucidation of the truth. At the same time, however, the ordinary

courtesies of debate oblige us to treat opinions of others with respect . . . To essay the overthrow of an opponent by a flood of
sarcastic criticism and personal invective is altogether unseemly, and
quite out of place either in writing or speaking on subjects pertaining
to science.

*Pencil drawing of Cleopatra (*Gonepteryx
cleopatra*), a butterfly rather like the brimstone which
occurs in southern Europe. This would have been sent to
Frohawk, probably as an egg or larva to breed out.*

One gains the impression that South was aiming these comments at a definite
target and from the very lengthy comments on exhibits reported in the *Proceedings*,
together with an overt desire to give the final answer to everything, one suspects
that the villain was Tutt. Although very energetic, intelligent and hard-working,
Tutt had a smooth personality and by his charm was able to gather information
from other people to use in his books. Perhaps Tutt's main role was as a compiler
of scattered information, which he did well. In Frohawk's obituary in *The
Entomologist* (1947) it was said that Tutt's 'reputation was achieved mainly by
means of a fluent pen, a somewhat vitriolic tongue and the labours of others.' The
issue was a personal one as South found Tutt difficult, and Frohawk and Tutt also
did not get on well. Frohawk ceased to attend meetings of the Society in 1897, for
the reason, perhaps, that he found the atmosphere uncongenial. In 1898 Tutt

*Pencil drawing to show the pattern of veins in
the wing of the grayling (*Hipparchia
semele*) male.*

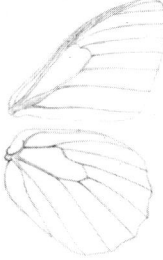

became President of the South London Entomological and Natural History Society, and the same year Frohawk resigned his membership. Tutt died in 1911 and it is of some significance that Frohawk rejoined the Society in 1912, immediately becoming an active member once more. He would have recognised many familiar faces at meetings from his earlier membership.

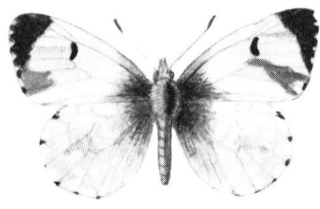

*Pencil and crayon drawing of the orange tip (*Anthocharis cardamines*), one of the common spring butterflies. It breeds on crucifers including lady's smock and hedge garlic in the wild and sweet rocket in gardens.*

In February 1912 Frohawk exhibited his drawing of a spotted mole that had been published in *The Field* the previous month. Meetings were still strongly centred around exhibits and discussion, although later more lectures were brought into the programme. By 1916 Frohawk was back on the council, and in the *Proceedings* for 1915 he contributed a paper on the birds of the Scilly Isles. In 1917 he was promoted to Vice-President, and after this he continued to serve on the council until 1922. Although he remained a member for the rest of his life, being elected an Honorary Member in 1943, there are no further references to him exhibiting at meetings nor accounts of him in the *Proceedings* after 1924. It appears that in his mid-60s when he moved to Sutton, Surrey, he took a less active part, although still going to the annual exhibition with his wife and daughter Valezina.

*Large heath (*Coenonympha tullia, *subspecies* scotica*). In Britain there are three local geographical races of this butterfly which are regarded as sub-species. This is the northern one from the Orkneys and Scotland.*

OTHER CONTACTS

Most of Frohawk's entomological papers and notes were published in the journal *The Entomologist*, and from his first contribution in 1882 he had something in virtually every volume until his last note in 1945, a year before he died. Some of the papers for *The Entomologist* were recast in a more popular form for *The Field*. In 1895 Frohawk was on the editorial board of *The Entomologist* with Richard South as overall editor.

Frohawk had a number of entomological friends, from both the amateur and professional worlds. Amongst these friends were John Wood, The Hon. Walter and Charles Rothschild, Douglas Forsyth Johnstone, Arthur Valentine (whose real name was Archibald Thomas Pechey), the Baron Bouck, W.A. Cope and Captain Purefoy. Douglas Forsyth Johnstone, with whom Frohawk used to go collecting in Essex, was not a member of the South London Entomological and Natural History Society, but his brother John ('Jack') was and the latter contributed an article on the Duke of Burgundy butterfly in Essex to *The Field* in 1912. Arthur Valentine, a novelist, dramatist and amateur entomologist, lived at Herne Bay, Kent, later moving to London, and he joined the Society in 1924. Baron Bouck lived at Godstone in Kent and around the 1920s Frohawk used to help him regularly with his entomological collection:

> From Beckenham I used to assist Baron Bouck (at his fine old house Springfield, S. Godstone) with his entomological collection 3 or 4 times weekly[1], but during the shooting season I accompanied him and had many days good sport especially with wild pheasants. After leaving Beckenham I continued going to Godstone from Carshalton. During the great strike in 1926 when no buses were running from Purley, I walked in hot weather from there to Godstone arriving there before noon. I continued going there until mid-April 1935 when the Baron went away on holiday for several weeks.

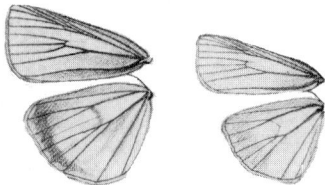

Drawing in pencil to show the veins in the wings of a butterfly.

[1]*Frohawk's daughter suggests that it was not as frequent.*

G. H. VERRALL.

1887   1911

Entomological Club

VERRALL SUPPER

Jubilee

1887 ‑ 1937

held at

THE HOLBORN RESTAURANT, KINGSWAY

on

TUESDAY, JANUARY 19th, 1937.

Every year a special dinner is held for entomologists known as the Verrall Supper, a tradition started in 1887. Frohawk was introduced to this function in 1890, and this is where he would meet, annually, the core of the British entomological world:

> When I first attended the meeting of Entomologists known as 'Verrall's meeting' in 1890 as guest of the late J.T. Carrington then the Editor of *The Entomologist*. I regularly attended this important gathering of entomologists from all parts of the British Isles for forty five years without a break, being a record. The late G.H. Verrall of Newmarket was of a most genial and kind nature. His big work on the British Diptera (two winged flies) is the standard work on the subject. Since his death in 1911 the meetings have been annually held at the Holborn Restaurant, London until the outbreak of the war, the last gathering being in January 1939.

Lists of those attending the Verrall Supper were given in *The Entomologist*.

FROHAWK AS ENTOMOLOGIST

Frohawk published regularly in *The Entomologist*, primarily on Lepidoptera, and also in the *Transactions of the Entomological Society of London* (later to become the Royal Entomological Society) and in *The Field*. He held a curious but central position in the entomological world, being an amateur yet working among professionals. In mid-Victorian times entomology, as all other branches of natural history, was mainly concerned with the collection of specimens and the study of identification and variation. Most amateur naturalists made collections, often of butterflies, and by so doing, learned about the insects they collected. In the last half of the nineteenth century, new universities were set up, and in these institutions zoology was based on the study of anatomy, adaptation and body function or physiology, as is explained in David Allen's book *The Naturalist in Britain* (1976). A rift therefore developed between amateurs and professionals at this time; each side was suspicious of the other and preferred to follow its own separate path. The 'new' biologists also used a good deal of jargon, perhaps intentionally, which prevented the amateur naturalists from understanding what they had to say. The rift widened as a result of this lack of communication.

Frohawk did not study at a university and had no official training or qualifications in biology or art. However, he was a naturally gifted and careful observer, very hard working and keen to learn. It was also his good fortune to come under

(Left) Menu card for the Verrall Supper in 1937. This annual event is a social meeting point for British entomologists. Frohawk attended on this occasion, but the Verrall Supper did not meet during the Second World War. Frohawk attended the post-war meeting shortly before he died.

*Caterpillar of the swallowtail moth (*Ourapteryx sambucaria*), which is camouflaged by resembling a twig.*

the wing of such well-established entomologists as Dr A.G. Butler and Dr Richard South and the Hon. Walter (later Lord) Rothschild of Tring. Working within the departments of the British Museum in South Kensington, particularly in the early years of his career, Frohawk would have absorbed a good deal of the approach of the professional entomologist, and his own interests in the subject also put him in the professional camp.

Whilst the amateur movement concentrated on collecting and identifying, Frohawk was more interested in studying the ways of life of butterflies in relation to their environment, an aspect of the subject which later came to be called ecology. His original work was divided between field observation and life cycle studies in captivity. The high standards he adopted earned him the acceptance of the professionals; such was his recognition that, while already elected a Fellow of the Entomological Society of London in 1891, he was honoured as a Special Life Fellow in 1926.

As well as achieving acceptance amongst the hierarchy of entomology, Frohawk was also revered by more general naturalists and had many amateur entomologists as personal friends. In his obituary in *The Entomologist* (1947) Dr N.D. Riley sums up by saying:

> so much was he for the last fifty years the hub around which amateur Lepidopterists gravitated, especially those interested chiefly in butterflies, that every bit of news seemed to find its way to him, to be examined, criticized and if suitable published.

To dear Mabel Jane with loving wishes for a happy birthday 21·4·42
from hubby.

Water-colour of spring flowers painted as a birthday card for his wife Mabel
Jane in 1942, when Frohawk was over eighty.

This attitude is born out by his daughter Valezina who, with her parents, used to attend the annual exhibition of the South London Entomological and Natural History Society. On the last occasion when he attended in 1946, a few months before he died, Frohawk was surrounded by members, all pleased to see him there.

Frohawk's memoir includes accounts of field work, which was one of his greatest interests in life, and the details remained clearly in his mind for many years. In his memoir, Frohawk recalls a day of butterfly collecting in Kent during 1885 with Edward Bartlett, the son of A.D. Bartlett the Superintendent of the London Zoological Gardens.

> He was Curator of the Maidstone Museum. When he was there I remember seeing four specimens of the Large Copper (dispar) in the Butterfly collection but after he left the museum, when I again viewed the collection they were not there. It was in August 1886 he and I went butterfly collecting to Chattenden, then belonging to Earl Darnley. The woods there were noted for the variety of insect life, a well known locality for the Purple Emperor. On that day in August we were the last collectors to see examples (two for certain) of this fine insect. It evidently became extinct that year in the Chattenden Woods, Kent.

Enquiries on the existence of the specimens of the large copper in the Maidstone Museum brought a reply from the present curator Eric Philp, who reports that all except one specimen are still there.

In spite of their beautiful appearance, butterflies can have unsavoury habits and a dung patch attracts many high fliers to ground level. The following notes were made in the 1940s when Frohawk was living in Galloway, Scotland:

> On July 9th I watched a Large Skipper butterfly feeding on a bird's dropping, the first one. Several kinds of butterflies are attracted to the dung of animals and other liquids for the purpose of feeding on the juices, and on many occasions I have found them imbibing the putrid exudations from the remains of animals. As is well known the beautiful Purple Emperor delights in feasting on putrid animal matter, also the Comma will feed on similar filth. I have seen the Chalk-hill Blue, the Holly Blue, the Wall and the White Admiral, the Green-veined White all feeding on horse dung. The first time I saw the White Admiral on horse dung was a long time ago in July 1872 on a roadway leading through a wood near Ipswich. It is a common habit of the Red Admiral, Holly Blue, all three species of Whites to drink at puddles on freshly watered roads. A curious habit I have noticed with the Dingy Skipper is excreting liquid and imbibing it by passing its tongue down between the legs. This butterfly will also feed on human perspiration. The renowned Dr. A.R. Wallace told me that the then unique Calliper Butterfly he found in Borneo was drinking at a puddle of dirty water.

*Pencil drawing of a silver-spotted skipper (*Hesperia comma*), a rare butterfly of chalk and limestone hills in southern England. The sole food of the caterpillar is the grass sheep's fescue (*Festuca ovina*).*

Frohawk's numerous notes published over a lifetime often comment on invasions of butterflies migrating to our shores and causing an enormous influx in numbers of such species as clouded yellow, Camberwell beauty, red admiral and painted lady. There was an invasion in Britain of clouded yellow in 1983.

> It is remarkable that the *greatest* invasions of the Painted Lady butterfly from abroad have occurred during these two wettest years on record (1879 and 1903).

Frohawk was always interested in linking animal behaviour with the weather. Each entomological season is different and Frohawk often published accounts of butterflies in different years. On one occasion at Hastings in 1928 he saw migrating butterflies coming in from the sea. The overwintering of butterflies and details of their life cycles were of particular interest and Frohawk was aware of the differences between species. Whereas some British butterflies, such as the brimstone, overwinter as hibernating adults others do not appear to be able to withstand the British winter. In *The Entomologist* and *The Field* Frohawk wrote about the non-hibernation of the red admiral in Britain, explaining that the presence of this butterfly is due to immigration.

Although the bulk of Frohawk's entomological work was on butterflies, he took

*Silver-washed fritillary (*Argynnis paphia*) from the New Forest, Hampshire, 23 July 1892. This butterfly, along with other species, has seriously declined in much of the New Forest.*

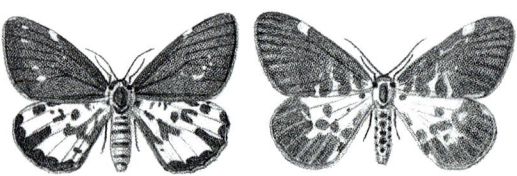

*Pencil drawing of a magpie moth (*Abraxas grossulariata*) to illustrate a paper by Robert Adkin in* The Entomologist, *1897. The specimen was bred from larvae collected near Fulham, South London. Caterpillars of this moth can be a pest on currants and gooseberries in gardens and it is sometimes known as the gooseberry moth.*

an interest in other groups and occasionally contributed notes on them to *The Field* or *The Entomologist*. Having such a long life, he was able to see how the abundance of the various species fluctuated over the years:

*The Scotch argus (*Erebia aethiops*), a northern butterfly which Frohawk saw in the field during his stay in Galloway. Painted for his daughter's birthday, 1941.*

*(Left) Small phoenix moth (*Ecliptopera silaceata*). Water-colour painting made 18 September 1885.*

*(Right) Water-colour of the caterpillar of the lime hawk moth (*Mimas tiliae*) drawn from life 1887. The spectacular caterpillars of the hawk moths draw much attention when they are found in gardens.*

There are two insects which have become so scarce or on the verge of extinction in certain localities during the past half century from some mysterious cause viz. the Musk Beetle and the beautiful Rose Beetle. During the 'seventies' the former was abundant in some places on the trunks of old willow trees. In the Crystal Palace grounds, round the boat-lake were a number of old pollard willows, at the end of the 'seventies' and early 'eighties'. I remember Musk Beetles were so numerous on these old trees that the scent of these beetles could be detected several yards away, but after the mid 'eighties' I saw no more of them, yet the trees remained the same. Also the disappearance applies to the river Wandle between Croydon and Beddington where they were common at that time. When living in Croydon from the autumn of 1873 to the autumn of 1876, at the bottom of the garden was a large oak tree. Each summer when the oak apples (galls) were young a large number of Rose Beetles seemed to be attracted by the galls, as I recollect daily seeing a lot of these beetles both on the foliage and flying around like bees. In the 'eighties' and 'nineties' they apparently became scarce and I cannot recall seeing one in Essex while living there between 1900 and 1911 and again from 1917 till 1923, nor in other counties visited. In 1926 I saw one specimen on the flower head of hemlock at Goodwood, Sussex. It is curious that both these beetles became rare at the same time.

Sometimes encounters with other groups, such as biting flies, were less than welcome as Frohawk recalls from the New Forest in 1888, whilst there with John Wood:

> Flies in annoying swarms were in constant attendance. The great *Tabanus bovinus* loudly buzzing round us and the detestable clegs running their needle-like proboscis into us were too numerous everywhere.

Even dedicated naturalists are human in cases like this! In spite of the flies, Frohawk had a respect for the insect world and their degree of adaptation to difficult conditions on land:

> It is a wonderful natural provision of life how minute insects can endure the burning rays of the midsummer sun, but they seem to revel in the heat. These animated atoms may be seen on slabs of metal, stone and other objects, resting or running about in perfect ease and comfort yet the surface is so heated by the sun that it is unbearable to our hands.

In spite of his declining health in later years, Frohawk was making discoveries to the end as the following quotation shows. (Claude Morley was a prominent member of the Suffolk Naturalists' Society.)

> I sent to Claude Morley (the authority on the ichneumonids) an ichneumon cocoon from *A. urticae* larvae 2nd Aug. 1941. This is a new species to me, the only one out of some thousands of *urticae* (Small Tortoiseshell) bred. The following is his reply 'The ichn. cocoon you send is that of *Phobocampa unicincta*, Grav. described in my *Ichn. Brit.* V 1914, 137 and bred in Germany from *Vanessa urticae* in 80, but apparently not from that host since then. Best thanks.' I also sent him

*High brown fritillary (*Argynnis adippe*). Formerly a woodland butterfly, but now almost restricted to a few rough hillsides. In Frohawk's time the species was locally abundant in rides and glades of the New Forest, Hampshire, where it is currently on the verge of extinction. The adult nectars on thistle and bramble flowers and the caterpillars feed on violets.*

a fine black ichneumon, with a white thoracic spot and middle of antennae white which I found in a semi-torpid state hibernating under damp birch bark on Nov. 18th 1940. This is his reply 'I am delighted to get your Ichn. from so far north; a rare sp. in Brit. . . . It is *Ichneumon lugens* Grav. and is known to hibernate but has *never* been bred (doubtless from Noctuae). Best thanks for the specimen.'

Noctuae are moths.

Frohawk made a collection of insects during his childhood in East Anglia which undoubtedly provided good learning experience and foundations for later study, for the mind of a keen child is very receptive. With time, he improved his technique in setting and, adding new specimens over the years, he built up a fine collection. For Frohawk, the collection was a useful tool for further study, rather than the be-all and end-all of entomology as it was for so many amateurs. However, the sportsman in him was still able to take pleasure in the capture of a

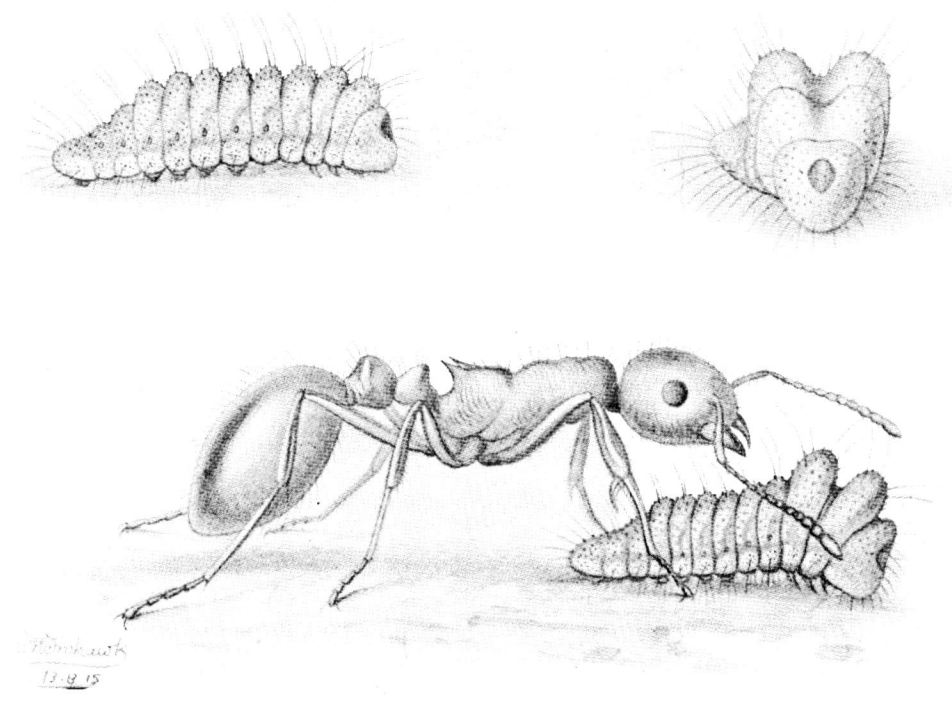

Prospectus for the Natural History of British Butterflies *with an illustration by Frohawk showing the ant carrying the larva of the large Blue* (Maculinea arion). *Frohawk's classic work was published in 1924.*

new rarity. The bulk of his butterfly collection, some 6,000 specimens, was sold to Lord Rothschild in 1927 for £1,000. This must have been a considerable sacrifice for Frohawk. The Walter Rothschild Collection, with Frohawk's butterflies incorporated in it, is now in the Department of Entomology of the British Museum (Natural History) in South Kensington.

According to his daughter Valezina, Frohawk made other collections and specimens were often given away to friends and colleagues. Those given to Lord Bolingbroke after Frohawk's death are now in the Bolingbroke Collection in the National Museum of Wales, Cardiff.

With his interests in distribution and fluctuating populations, Frohawk's butterfly collection is particularly valuable from a scientific point of view for its full details of locality and dates of collection. So many amateur collections were deficient in this information and, however attractive and well presented, could be of no lasting value to the serious entomologist. Frohawk did not believe in buying his specimens from dealers, and most of those in his collection would have been caught by himself or bred from larvae or eggs. He did acquire a few old collections which he valued for their locality data, and he sometimes quoted from these in his entomological notes in *The Field* and *The Entomologist*, as evidence of the former distributions of species.

9

The Butterfly Books

Frohawk's butterfly books, particularly the *Natural History of British Butterflies*, were the highlight of his career but, being the culmination of many years of work, they were not published until the later years of his life. In these books three skills – careful natural history observation, artwork and writing – were brought together in a project of his own inspiration.

THE NATURAL HISTORY OF BRITISH BUTTERFLIES

Although the large two-volume *Natural History of British Butterflies* was not published until Frohawk was 63 years of age, the project was begun some 30 years

The purple emperor (Apatura iris, form iola Schiff), published as Plate 1 in Varieties of British Butterflies *(1938). The specimen was captured by J. Waters, July 1866, in Chattenden Woods, Kent, and was from the F.W. Frohawk Collection.*

earlier. It was an ambitious task, as Frohawk set out to study the life cycle, feeding habits and ecology of all the British species of butterflies and to provide material for original illustrations from egg to imago, involving a massive programme of captive breeding. Stages of some of the life cycles had never before been illustrated. This was all undertaken in Frohawk's spare time, alongside the usual commissioned work that paid the household bills, so the time-span involved in the large butterfly book is not surprising. What is surprising is that Frohawk managed to cover so much ground and original research. In his memoir, he recalls the beginning of the work for his first butterfly book:

> In 1890 I started rearing British Butterflies through all their stages for the purpose of working out their complete life-histories, to enable me to describe and figure every stage of every species, which occupied twenty-four years. One species, the Large Blue baffled all previous attempts to fathom its mysterious history which I succeeded in accomplishing doing after eleven years investigation, which is looked upon as the greatest entomological achievement. The book was at last published in 1924 in two 4to volumes, containing 1,500 coloured drawings which became the property of Lord Rothschild who be-queathed them to the nation. In 1934, my second work on British Butterflies was published, entitled the *Complete Book of British Butter-flies* one vol. and in 1938 my third volume appeared on *Varieties of British Butterflies* containing 48 coloured plates.

*An aberrant form of the Scotch argus (*Erebia aethiops*) captured at Carnforth, 1894. This illustration was published in* The Complete Book of British Butterflies *(1934)*

In the introduction to the *Natural History of British Butterflies*, Frohawk points out that before 1890 it was thought that butterflies would not lay eggs in captivity and this erroneous belief discouraged entomologists from attempting to breed them. Once it was discovered that captive breeding was possible many entomologists, particularly in the South London Entomological and Natural History Society, became involved in this work.

Frohawk was quick to see the potential for a whole area of study which could arise from the systematic breeding of species, describing and illustrating all the different stages. While the outline of the life history was known for some

*Chalkhill blue (*Lysandra coridon*). Common locally on rough chalk and limestone hillsides where horseshoe vetch (*Hippocrepis comosa*) is present as a food plant for the larvae.*

butterflies, others had not been fully investigated before and, because so many natural history books at that time were based on pre-existing publications, unchecked errors were passed from book to book. Edward Thomas, the early twentieth century topographical writer and poet, refers to the same problem in his experience when books are 'made out of books, founded on other books'. Like Frohawk, Edward Thomas preferred to write directly from his own experience of the countryside, rather than summarise the impressions of others.

The road which led to the first butterfly book was a long and arduous one, for any work involving keeping cultures of animals alive over long periods is time-consuming and demanding. To breed butterflies, the entomologist first had to capture already mated females which, when provided with the right plant, could be induced to lay eggs in captivity. The butterfly was contained in a net cage placed over the plant. The eggs would then hatch and be reared through the caterpillar and chrysalid stages to the adult butterfly. To do this it was necessary to know the right plant for both egg-laying and feeding the caterpillars. Regular observation was necessary to be able to illustrate all the stages, and sometimes specimens had to be watched day and night over considerable lengths of time. Life cycles of butterflies take 8 to 10 months to be completed, and breeding all the British species took 24 years of Frohawk's lifetime, during which at least 900 drawings were made of the juvenile stages alone.

The project had a slow start due to 'pecuniary embarrassment' and the impossibility of devoting more than a small proportion of his time to it. During the 1890s Frohawk married and started a family, which increased his financial responsibilities and outgoings, and he also became involved in an abortive project to set up a zoo in Brighton (described in Chapter 5). This collapsed in 1899, leaving him without funds or employment.

*Short-tailed blue (*Everes argiades*). This is a rare casual migrant to Britain and, like other blues, it probably has a short adult life.*

*The red admiral (*Vanessa atalanta, *form* albo-punctura*). The specimen had been bred in captivity by B.P. Kemp from a larva found at Erith, Kent in 1889. From E. Sabine's collection.*

From 1900, however, progress on the butterfly books was accelerated:

> The munificence of Lord Rothschild did much to accelerate and facilitate the progress of the work, and the author, who desires here to record an expression of his deep indebtedness, has no hesitation in saying that without Lord Rothschild's assistance and encouragement his prolonged, and at times tedious, task could never have attained to completion.

Lord Rothschild, who was one of the partners in the failed Brighton zoo project, may have felt some responsibility for the situation in which Frohawk found himself in 1899 and helped to sponsor the book. He also bought the original artwork for it, so this, as part of the Rothschild bequest, is now in the Department of Entomology of the British Museum (Natural History).

Throughout the project various observations and illustrations made for the book were published, mostly in *The Field*. By 1914 both the text and the paintings were complete and Lord Rothschild provided a preface. However, the First World War broke out and the publication of the book was delayed. *The Field*, as a welcome break from unpleasant news of the war, published much of the substance

(Right) Colour plate from the Natural History of British Butterflies *(1924) showing the stages of the life history of the peacock butterfly,* Nymphalis io *that breeds on the stinging nettle* Urtica diocia. *(Reproduced with permission of the British Museum (Natural History) who hold the original artwork.)*

of the book together with its illustrations (black-and-white only) in serial form starting in December 1914. During wartime, the quality of paper available was limited and this was reflected in the appearance of *The Field* in the later war years.

The First World War ended in 1918, but it was not until 1924 that the *Natural History of British Butterflies* by F.W. Frohawk was published, and various other factors may have been operative in its delay. The post-war depression of the economy and the decline in number of amateur naturalists (many having been killed in action), together with the weakened state of most of the natural history societies at this time, would have severely limited the market for the book. The publishing climate at the time was not favourable and Hutchinson, the publisher, invited subscribers and published the more prominent of the 200 names on the dust jacket and a full list at the end of Volume 2. It is doubtful whether Frohawk gained much financially from his life's work.

How did this book differ from previous books on British butterflies and achieve the status of an entomological classic? Much of the explanation can be found in Lord Rothschild's preface and in the introduction to Volume 1. There had been many previous books on British butterflies which were based on identification and variation of form, but these gave the natural history aspect only limited treatment. Furthermore, many of the standard references were compilations from other works, whereas Frohawk's book was completely original. He personally observed and checked nearly all the statements that went into the book, and the whole project was based on his long-term breeding programme and extensive experience of butterflies in the field. The uneven state of knowledge on the life cycles of the different species meant that Frohawk was able to describe and figure many stages for the first time. Nobody has since attempted such a single-handed programme of research on the British butterfly fauna, and the *Natural History of British Butterflies*

Adonis blue (Lysandra bellargus). *A rare and distinctive brilliant blue butterfly occurring on short turf on chalk and limestone, particularly in the south-east. Like the chalkhill blue, the larvae feed on horseshoe vetch.*

Mazarine blue (Cyaniris semiargus). *This species was once plentiful in a few localities in southern Britain in the nineteenth century and specimens exist in old collections. It is now extinct in Britain.*

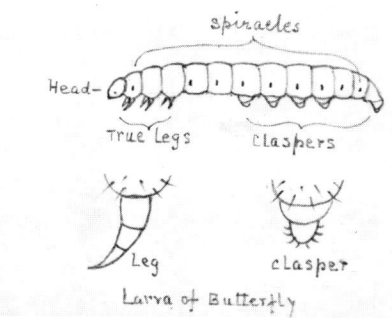

Pencil drawing of a caterpillar showing the parts of the body that was drawn for The Complete Book of British Butterflies *(1934).*

remains a classic tome of reference to lepidopterists over sixty years after it was first published.

The book is also unusual in that the research, writing and illustrations were all Frohawk's own work. The careful water-colour drawings were outstanding and included such detail as day-old caterpillars that have never been published by other authors. As well as being informative and accurate, they were very beautiful plates. The *Natural History of British Butterflies* cost £6 6s and was therefore an expensive publication and not likely to find its way on to the shelves of the majority of naturalists of modest means. Today, second-hand copies sell at around £200.

FROHAWK AND THE LARGE BLUE

One of Frohawk's greatest achievements in entomology was the part he played in the elucidation of the life cycle of the large blue butterfly, then a rare species and now extinct in Britain. The wartime delay in the publication of his book enabled the full story of the large blue to be solved and incorporated in the text. In the 1880s the large blue, formerly an uncommon species, was thought to be on the verge of extinction, but in 1891 E.A. Waterhouse found it to be quite abundant on the north-west coast of Cornwall. Frohawk visited the county following his discovery in quest of the large blue.

*Large blue (*Maculinea arion*). Frohawk was instrumental in elucidating the role of the ant in the life cycle of the large blue. It was then a rare species but has since been declared extinct in Britain in 1979.*

The orange tip (Anthocharis cardamines). *The left one, from the collection at Tring Museum, was found at Chingford Mount in 1898 but was not used in* Varieties. *The other is one of four figures in Plate 41, the form* macula-punctata, *a specimen captured at Horsley, Surrey, in June 1892, from the F.W. Frohawk Collection.*

Another noteworthy naturalist I personally knew intimately was Mr. E.A. Waterhouse (brother of Mr. E.O. Waterhouse of entomological fame, of the Brit. Museum). The episode concerning the discovery of the Large Blue on the north-west coast of Cornwall in July 1891, is so remarkable, that it is worthy of mention. I may state this beautiful species suddenly became much rarer after the 70's where it occurred commonly on the Devon coast, on the Cotswolds, and Ashton and Barnwold, Northamptonshire and was considered to be on the verge of extinction in Britain until Mr. Waterhouse's discovery. I will give it as told to me by Mr. Waterhouse who was on an exploration holiday in unfrequented places in the countryside, and anxious to know of the local fauna and flora of the localities he visited. Arriving at a rural spot south of Bude he managed to put up at the only cottage there was then available (25/- per week inclusive of *very* good meals). After a good nights rest, when he had a pleasant dream of catching three examples of the Large Blue in his wanderings, he thought no more about it. The following morning being dull with rain at times he strolled about with the object of doing some botanical work so took his botanical tin, and a butterfly net in case of it getting finer. To his astonishment, he had not gone far, he saw and caught one of these butterflies. This so surprised him that he kept a sharp look out for more, and succeeded in catching two more. Having caught the three specimens of his previous nights dream, and again turning dull with rain about to fall, he returned to his room at the cottage to mediate over the queer coincidence. The next day being fine he was rewarded by catching several others where subsequently they proved to be abundant.

(Right) The habitat, food plant and life history of the high brown fritillary (Argynnis adippe). *This water-colour was commissioned by the British Museum (Natural History) for publication as a postcard and later in a booklet for sale at the Museum.*

The large blue used to appear in June and lay its eggs on the flower heads of wild thyme during July. The caterpillars at first fed exclusively on thyme flowers until the third moult, but thereafter it seemed to suddenly disappear, and there was a gap in the knowledge of the life cycle. This was a puzzle and several entomologists grappled with it. The mystery was finally solved and published in a series of articles in the *Transactions of the Entomological Society of London* from 1915 to 1916.

Frohawk discovered that the hibernating caterpillar was in its final instar (i.e. fully grown). Dr T.A. Chapman also followed up the story and in 1915 found the large blue caterpillar associated with the nest of an ant (*Myrmica scabrinodis* – the elbowed red ant) and that the mature caterpillars were feeding on ant larvae. In a further paper published the same year Chapman postulated on the association between the ant and the caterpillar and gave a description of the caterpillar swelling up before it was seized by the ant and carried to the nest. This was discovered in collaboration with Mr Donisthorpe, using reared larvae and an observation ants' nest – Frohawk supplied the eggs.

Frohawk, together with his friend Captain Purefoy, experimented with artificial ants' nests that were established in Purefoy's garden at East Farleigh, Kent. The first observations on the ant and the large blue caterpillar in the vicinity of the transplanted ants' nest were made by Frohawk, Captain Purefoy and Miss Ley just two weeks after the outbreak of the First World War in August 1914: they observed several larvae being taken to the nest by the ant (*Myrmica laevinodis* another red ant). In October that year they opened the ants' nest and found some healthy large blue larvae inside. They also tried the experiment using *Lasius flavus* (the yellow meadow ant) which did not prove to be a suitable host, explaining why Frohawk had failed to find the caterpillar in the nest of this species of ant that he had searched in Cornwall. Frohawk's fine drawing showing the ant picking up the larva of the large blue was published in his paper in the *Transactions of the Entomological Society of London* (1916).

Accounts of the large blue in both the *Natural History of British Butterflies* (1924) and the later *Complete Book of British Butterflies* (1934) show that Frohawk studied the butterfly in the field in 1902, and noticed that they always seemed to occur around ant hills supporting wild thyme. He postulated at that time on a possible connection between the ant and the butterfly, but the answer took another twelve years to find.

Studies on the large blue butterfly involved much arduous work in the field. Writing in *The Entomologist* in 1906, Frohawk records discoveries made during his visit to Cornwall with A.L. Rayward the previous summer. As well as searching for the elusive immature stages of the large blue in the daytime, they sat up at night, searching by lamplight. In the hunt they dug up many ants' nests and were eventually rewarded with a larva which they found by shaking the crown of an ants' nest over a cloth. At this time they were also able to observe a larva pupating.

Some of Frohawk's drawings were started in the field, and in his review of the *Natural History of British Butterflies* in 1925 N.D. Riley explained that the sketch of the ant carrying the larva of the large blue necessitated Frohawk kneeling on the ground for an hour or more with a lens in one hand and a pencil in the other.

THE COMPLETE BOOK OF BRITISH BUTTERFLIES

Frohawk's second book, *The Complete Book of British Butterflies*, was published by Ward Lock in 1934. Whilst the first book was an expensive specialist monograph, the second aimed at the broader market of the general naturalist. This concise volume also concentrated on life cycles and biology but, being a later publication, brought information on the status and distribution of species up to date. It was again based on personal experience and original work and is full of interesting and authentic facts about British butterflies.

The Complete Book of British Butterflies was illustrated with both monochrome text figures and colour plates and since Lord Rothschild had bought the paintings for the first book, a completely new set of illustrations was prepared for the second one. The introductory section included text on aberrations and their possible protective function, migrations of butterflies (which are important in explaining the abundance of certain species from time to time), hints on collecting, rearing butterflies from the egg (something which Frohawk had been doing for many years) and a most useful list of food plants of different larvae to help in setting up breeding experiments.

VARIETIES OF BRITISH BUTTERFLIES

Four years later, in 1938, the last of the butterfly books, entitled *Varieties of British Butterflies*, was published by Ward Lock. While the previous books were geared to the field naturalist, the third title was for the collector who was particularly

*An aberrant form of the dark green fritillary (*Argynnis aglaja*) captured in the New Forest, Hampshire, 1893. This illustration was published in* The Complete Book of British Butterflies *(1934).*

*The dark green fritillary (*Argynnis aglaja, *the right-hand one is form* ater-discus)*, published as Plate 14 in* Varieties. *Both specimens were from the Rothschild Collection and captured at Brighton, Sussex, the left-hand one on 3 July 1900 and the right-hand one on 9 July 1899.*

*Pale clouded yellow (*Colias hyale)*, an albino (left) and form* ater-marginata *(right). These are two of the three figures in Plate 12 in* Varieties. *The albino was captured by A. Griffiths on 1 September 1901 at Sheerness, Kent, and was from the F.W. Frohawk Collection. The other form was captured by F.A. Baley in August 1892 on Wimbledon Common, South London. From the Rothschild Collection (ex. E.A. Waterhouse Collection).*

*(Right) The habitat, food plant and life history of the cinnabar moth (*Tyria jacobaea)*. This water-colour was commissioned by the British Museum (Natural History) for publication as a postcard and later in a booklet for sale at the Museum. This day-flying moth breeds on ragworts and the caterpillars often completely defoliate their food plant.*

interested in abnormal forms. Accompanying the plates were notes summarising aberrations in the various species and these indicate changes in the incidence of variants from year to year. Full locality and collection data were also given for the specimens illustrated.

This richly illustrated book with 48 colour plates was Frohawk's last butterfly book and, with the possible exception of birds for *British Birds* published post-humously, this was his last big illustrating contract. Frohawk was already 77 years of age when it was published and the precision of the work is remarkable. However, the many years of long hours doing detailed work had begun to tell and by then he had great problems with his eyesight and had to give up commissioned work.Sadly, the original artwork for two books was destroyed in the Second World War, as Frohawk explains:

> The whole bound stock of books including both my books on Butter-flies *The Complete Book of British Butterflies* and *Varieties of British Butterflies* and all pertaining to them have been lost by the destruction of Warwick House, by the disastrous fire caused by a bomb on the last Sunday night of 1940, owing to the terrible raid on London. Fortu-nately the coloured drawings done for my forthcoming book on British Birds were put into the stone safe only a few days previously. Colour blocks of 40 coloured sketches of the 'soft parts' of birds have been destroyed. These would have been a valuable addition to the book, but all are lost. This is a serious loss to me, no more royalties forthcoming and nothing to be done in the near future.

This marked the end of a long career in natural history illustrating and writing.

FROHAWK'S CONTRIBUTION

Frohawk's work on butterflies was his greatest contribution to the scientific world but it was not financially rewarding, and, as he lived by illustrating books for other people, the butterfly research had to be fitted into his limited spare time.

Throughout Frohawk's writings there are accounts of changes in butterfly populations and this fluctuation continues today. Some like the high brown fritillary and large tortoiseshell are endangered; others like the holly blue continue to fluctuate in cycles; migrants like the clouded yellow, painted lady and red admiral come to Britain in some years but not others; while the comma, which was restricted to Herefordshire, Monmouthshire and Worcestershire in the early part of the twentieth century, is now much more common and widespread.

Although the garden butterflies are well provided for and reasonably numer-ous, some of the more interesting butterflies, which have rather precise habitat requirements, are plunging towards extinction in Britain. For example, the large blue on which Frohawk did so much work is now extinct in Britain. The position we find ourselves in with butterflies today is due in part to the great changes in land-use in the countryside, with greater mechanisation and production, that have destroyed vast areas of butterfly habitats and breeding sites. The few populations left are becoming increasingly isolated, as a result of which they become genetically inbred and lack the vigour to survive. John Muggleton and Brian Benham have suggested in their paper in *Biological Conservation* (1975) that fragmentation of distribution and genetic isolation are the prime causes of the disappearance of the large blue from Britain.

It is in sorting out problems of butterfly conservation that Frohawk's careful account of the biology of butterflies is most useful, indicating the conditions they need to survive and providing first-hand accounts of flourishing colonies of butterflies that are now rare. Frohawk's work is more relevant now than it has ever been.

Butterflies have always been popular with naturalists and collectors, but nowadays there is a strong trend towards their conservation, led by the British Butterfly Conservation Society and the Government's Nature Conservancy Council. The butterfly net and the killing bottle of the past are used much more sparingly and today's naturalists collect photographs instead of specimens. Butterflies have also seized the imagination of the tourist industry, and butterfly farms are springing up everywhere.

*Hawaiian honey creeper (*Loxops aurea = Himatione aurea*). Water-colour sketches from specimens in the British Museum, which were developed as a lithographic plate for* Aves Hawaiiensis: The Birds of the Sandwich Islands *by Wilson and Evans (1890–1899).*

10

Studies on Birds

FROHAWK AND SHOOTING

An interest in birds was a heritage of Frohawk's country childhood. As a boy, he probably made a collection of birds' eggs, while the trophies of the shooting parties at Brisley Hall would have enabled him to see freshly shot birds at close hand and to appreciate the detail in plumage that would not be visible at a distance in the field.

As a young man Frohawk was introduced to the sport of shooting, something which he indulged in from time to time throughout his life. Sportsmen were often good naturalists, since a knowledge of birds and their behaviour gave a greater chance of success at the shoot. Whilst waiting for birds, they were able to appreciate the countryside, the open air, interesting skies and wildlife, such as is described in the books of B.B. (D.J. Watkins-Pitchford), which reflect the atmosphere of the life of the sportsman-naturalist. In the present conservation-conscious age, naturalists are a little surprised at the shooting activities of their predecessors, which even included the Selborne naturalist Gilbert White, who had the reputation of a most gentle nature. However, shooting was a normal part of life in which the country gentleman was expected to take part. Birds which Frohawk had shot were often dissected, and the contents of the crop provided evidence of their feeding habits. Gilbert White also followed this line of investigation, as he took an interest in the feeding habits of birds too.

In his shooting area in Essex, Frohawk also made observations on the natural history of the birds:

> The lapwings were unmolested and I spent many hours (or rather days) observing their habits in November 1904 till the spring of 1905, I paid particular attention to them. In mid-November the flock numbered about 40 birds, but daily increased to about 1,000 in mid-February. They roosted in a ploughed field, until it was dark they kept up a chorus of bubbling-like notes. In the daytime, especially a fine sunny day, the great flock used to take long flights around. When high up with sun shining brightly they presented a very effective spectacle, their black and white plumage sparkling in the sunlight. Suddenly the great flock would wheel to earth. They were invariably followed by a flock of about 100 Golden Plover. It was then that I discovered the great sexual difference of the wings of this common

Pencil drawing of a wildfowl shoot on the coast. This was probably intended for a magazine illustration.

bird, the male having the wing very broad at the end, the 1st and 7th primaries being equal in the male, while in the female the 1st and 4th primaries are equal. This discovery made quite a stir in the ornithological world. I figured and described the sexual differences of the bills, crests and wings in *The Ibis* and *The Field* at the time. After lecturing on the subject and exhibiting specimens at a meeting of the British Ornithological Union, the Chairman remarked 'it shows what a lot there is to be learnt about the common birds'.

As an artist, Frohawk put shooting to good use as a means of providing him with specimens, especially when he visited the Scilly Isles. Here he saw a whole range of exciting sea birds – shag, razorbill, storm petrel, puffin and Manx shearwater – that were not to be found in his normal haunts of south-east England. He used his gun to obtain samples of each of them and made drawings and water-colour studies, which included details of heads, bills and feet, that could be used for future reference in commissioned work.

A collection of bird studies by Frohawk is now in the British Museum (Natural

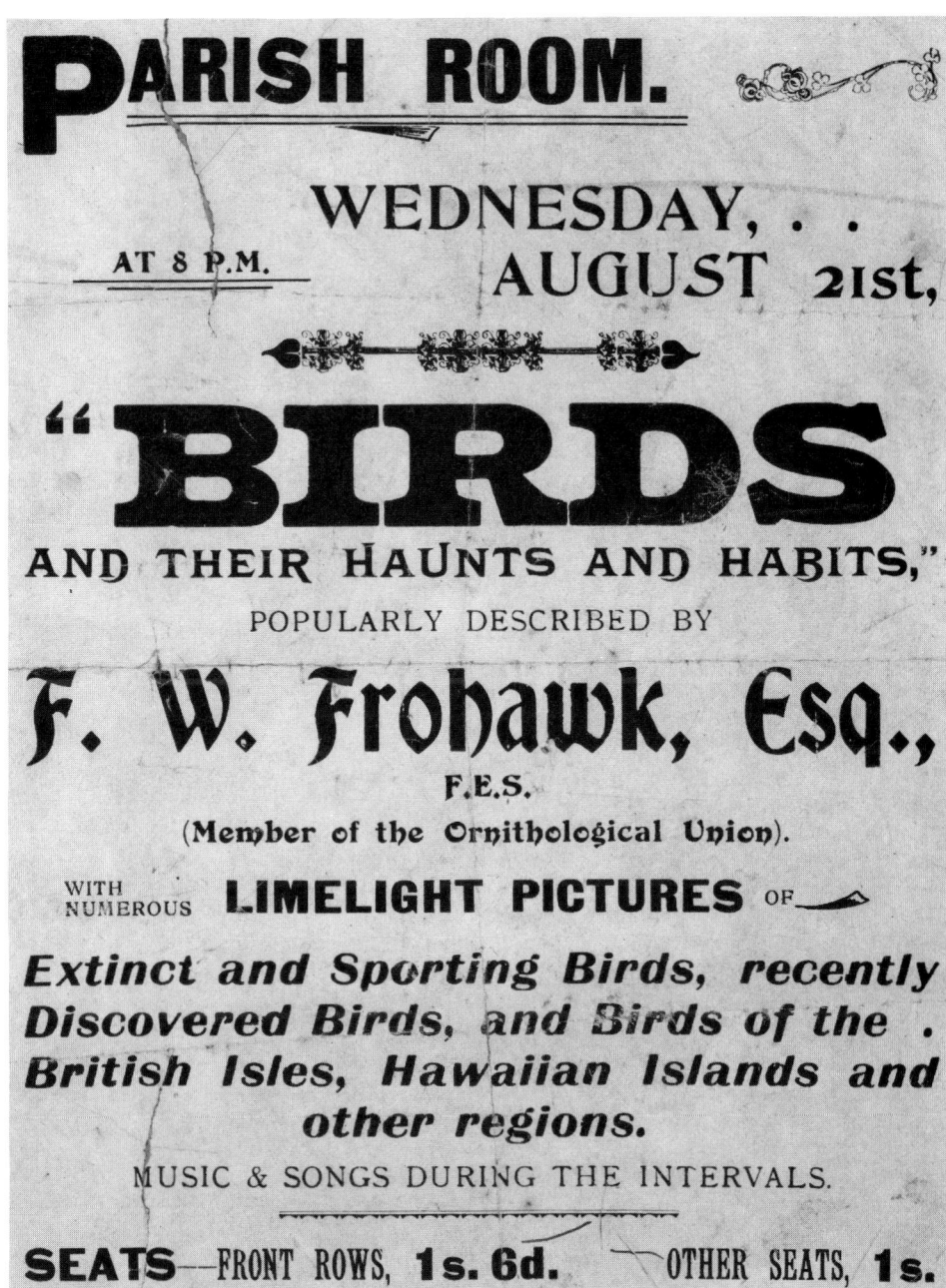

Poster advertising a lecture on birds given by Frohawk in Essex some time during the first quarter of the present century when he lived in that area.

*Mannikins (*Munia melana. M. forbes *and* M. spectabilis*).
Preliminary drawings in water-colour for book illustration.*

*(Top left) Indigo bunting, a pair with the male blue. A preliminary water-
colour for* Foreign Finches in Captivity *by A.G. Butler.*

*(Bottom left) The Carolina crake (*Porrana carolina carolina*); an
unfinished drawing in pencil and wash in preparation for an illustration
published in* The Field *in 1901.*

History). As biological records, they are also valuable for the annotations giving date and place of collection. From the Scilly Isles are sketches of sanderling, herring gull, lesser black-backed gull, turnstone, purple sandpiper, razorbill, great northern diver, bar-tailed godwit, shag, cormorant, curlew and common tern. The cormorant shot on 30 June 1909 was recorded as being sketched directly after death, while still on board the boat.

BIRD STUDIES

Frohawk described some of his bird studies on the Scilly Isles in the *Proceedings of the South London Entomological and Natural History Society* (1915–16):

> In the Scillies I spent a considerable time in studying the habits of this bird [the shearwater], and purposely passed a night on Annet in order to observe their movements during the few hours of darkness in early June. I landed on this wild island on the evening of June 3rd, 1904, and spent such a memorable night among the host of sea birds that it was an experience and pleasure never to be forgotten and rivals description. The spot selected to pass the night was one of the highest parts of the island, and which turned out to be the most suitable site, as every part of the ground was honeycombed with their nesting burrows. Up till 9.45 p.m. the time was mostly occupied by watching the movements of the puffins, which continued leaving and returning to their nests as long as the twilight lasted. At 9.45 I took up my position for the night. After waiting a few minutes the shearwater commenced crowing to each other underground, which produced a very weird effect in the darkness. Suddenly, at ten o'clock, they all appeared to leave the burrows at the same time, they emerged so quickly that for a minute or two they fluttered around in a great swarm, in the dim light I could just see their dark forms flapping about over the surface of the ground trying to rise, which they are unable to do without the aid of some hillock or other eminence from which to take flight. Very soon afterwards the air was filled with a dense swarm of these queer birds, flying round and round, crowing loudly, the noise they made by their remarkable cries was so great that the roar of the sea beating against the rocks only 30 or 40 yards away was drowned by the uproar they made. This wonderful assemblage of shearwaters kept up the flight and screaming for just three hours, when, at 1 a.m. precisely, there suddenly became silence, as if caused by some word of command, and the whole multitude went to sea, where they again set up their perpetual cries and continued until just before dawn, when they were heard no more. Apparently they all went to some distant fishing ground to return again at sundown, as at that time they are generally to be seen flying over the surface of the water round the islands, or careering along in a direct line homewards.

'Fearlessness of the Manx Shearwater. A wild bird on the Author's arm. 4
a.m., 4th June 1904.' Self-portrait in pencil originally published in the
Proceedings of the South London Entomological and Natural
History Society *(1915–1916). This would have been done on the Scilly Isles*
where the Manx shearwater occurs: these birds are nocturnal and are on the
wing at dusk; they breed in burrows in the cliffs of marine islands.

Among the same set of bird studies are some made from birds shot at Wallasea
and Rayleigh in Essex from 1903 to 1918 – eider duck, heron, redshank, dunlin,
golden plover, green sandpiper and green woodpecker – which represented birds
of quite different habitats compared to those of the Scilly Isles. Frohawk also went

shooting on Romney Marsh in Kent where he took jack snipe, teal, coot and common snipe.

These detailed studies of birds were clearly done for his own reference, to give accurate detailed information for use in later commissioned work. Perhaps his wash drawings for Butler's *British Birds with their Nests and Eggs* (1896–98) had alerted him to the need for extra detailed study when his work had to encompass the whole British bird list.

Working drawings of birds (in colour) were clearly part of a steady programme of Frohawk's work in the first two decades of the twentieth century. This series of working drawings is reminiscent of the 'feather maps' made by the later bird artist C.F. Tunnicliffe in the mid-twentieth century. Tunnicliffe was not a sportsman, in fact he took a firmly anti-shooting view, and he obtained his material for post-mortem drawings from dead and sometimes decomposing birds found on the beach at Anglesey, by the roadside or those brought to him. A large collection of Tunnicliffe's working drawings was recently bought by Mostyn Art Gallery, Anglesey (where the artist lived happily for the latter part of his life) and these were exhibited at the National Museum of Wales, Cardiff, in 1980. It is interesting to compare them with Frohawk's work.

The coloured bird drawings made for reference by both Frohawk and Tunnicliffe are accurate in every detail, carefully drawn to scale and annotated with measurements. Both artists were able to infuse life into the drawings they made from stiff bird corpses and they were both familiar with the characteristic postures

One of a series of water-colour studies showing the detail of feet and bills of birds made for future reference. This one is the curlew sandpiper, a male bird shot for study by Frohawk on the Scilly Isles, 2 September 1897. It is annotated with measurements: 'expanse 15 in, length 7¾in, wing 5⅛in, weight 2 oz.'

Preliminary sketch in water-colour wash and pencil of Hutchin's goose that was developed as a colour plate (No. 19) in The Geese of Europe and Asia *by Prince Alpheraky published in English in 1905. The illustration was made in 1902.*

and behaviour of the various species, and were thus able to produce authentic bird portraits.

Frohawk was a good field ornithologist and he saw some interesting rarities and varieties which were reported in notes to *The Field*, sometimes accompanied by illustrations. He also took particular note of aspects of bird behaviour, commenting on nesting habits, unusual numbers of eggs, bird song, feeding habits and movement. One unusual note concerned a house martins' nest next to a wasps' nest on the gardener's house at Wisley, both nests being occupied.

BOOK ILLUSTRATIONS

Birds were an important part of Frohawk's professional work as an artist, and the majority of the books he illustrated were on birds:

> Prof Alfred Newton, head of Magdalene College, Cambridge was a very noted ornithologist. In 1887 he sent me a wood drawing which other artists failed to satisfy him with the expression of the curious bird known as the Crested Screamer. This I happened to correct to his thorough satisfaction which led him to employ me to do the remaining drawings to accompany his articles on birds for the *Encyclopaedia Britannica*.

Frohawk is referring here to the ninth edition 1875–1889. Frohawk had already contributed drawings of reptiles and amphibians to the *Encyclopaedia Britannica* for Dr Gunther. It was through Professor Newton of Cambridge that Frohawk was asked to illustrate Scott B. Wilson's book, *Aves Hawaiiensis: Birds of the Sandwich Islands*.

From the late 1880s Frohawk started a series of commissions to illustrate bird books for Edward Bartlett (1888–89), Scott B. Wilson and A.H. Evans (1890–99), the Hon. Walter Rothschild (1893–1900), A.G. Butler (1894–1898), W.B. Tegetmeier (1897), Prince Alpheraky (1905), translated from Russian, and G.M. Mathews (1928). With the exception of Butler's book, these were all on foreign birds and Frohawk had to draw them mostly from flat skins, mounted museum specimens or sometimes live examples in captivity. Walter Rothschild kept a number of live birds at Tring.

In 1895 Frohawk joined the British Ornithologists' Union (B.O.U.), whose journal, *The Ibis*, published the *Proceedings* of the British Ornitholigists' Club. With between 20 and 35 members present, the club met at a restaurant in London. Walter Rothschild and W.B. Tegetmeier were both members, and both attended and exhibited at meetings; it was probably through one of them that Frohawk joined the B.O.U. Walter Rothschild did not always attend the meetings, but often sent one of his curators along with an exhibit. Frohawk remained a members of the B.O.U. until 1924, but there is no indication in the *Proceedings* of him taking an active part in meetings or committee, as he did with the South London Entomological and Natural History Society. Receipt of *The Ibis* would have kept him up to date with new books published on birds and he also illustrated some of the papers published in the journal. Frohawk did, however, attend some of the ornithological congresses, as he records in his memoir:

> At the fifth Ornithological Congress held in 1905, both my wife Margaret and myself were elected members. We met many of the most distinguished ornithologists from different parts of the world.

Frohawk's first wife, Margaret, standing beside his large painting of the moa (Dinornis ingens) *exhibited at the museum at Tring during the Ornithological Congress in 1905. The painting was reproduced in Lord Rothschild's book* Extinct Birds, *published 1907.*

The week was spent visiting different places of importance, the lectures were held in London. One meeting at Lord Rothschild's Tring Park where he held an exhibition of paintings of extinct birds for his great 25 guinea book of 'Extinct and Vanishing Birds'. My life-size water colour drawing of the Moa (*Dinornis ingens*) which stood 11 ft. 6 in. high, done on a great sheet of paper of 16 ft was the largest drawing there, and attracted the admiration of many visitors present; when I was introduced as the artist, I was surrounded by a gathering mass of foreigners bowing to me and shaking hands in appreciation of the greatness of the work. Another day the meeting was held at Woburn Abbey, the country seat of the Duke of Bedford. This was a great day. Most of the guests were driven in a team of carriages (then before the general use of motor-cars) from the station to the Abbey. There were twenty-five carriages, and the pairs of bays, the attendants all in brown and gold, the whole turn out resembling a regiment of soldiers while driving along the road, presenting quite a picturesque spectacle as the procession passed along. The lunch was held in the great banqueting hall, 250 sat down to lunch presided by the Duchess, the late Duke not being present, and the present Duke was then only 15 years of age. The tables were elaborately laid with large gold epergnes down the centre of each. I thought then what destruction of bird life when *each* guest was served with a quail, meaning 250 of these beautiful and beneficial little birds to be slaughtered for a single banquet. How many more are destroyed to provide for similar functions throughout the British Isles and elsewhere in Europe? During the afternoon we viewed the waterfowl on the lakes.

Crimson-headed weaver, preliminary water-colour for Foreign Finches in Captivity *by A.G. Butler. The bird comes from Africa.*

Saffron finch from South America. Again a preliminary water-colour for Foreign Finches in Captivity.

It was appropriate that an exhibition of Frohawk's work was on display at the National Museum of Wales during the annual conference of the B.O.U. at Cardiff in 1984.

Most of Frohawk's notes and articles on birds were published in *The Field* during the time he was natural history editor. In the circles of the South London Entomological and Natural History Society, he wore the hat of ornithologist as

Pencil sketch of a marsh tit and a hawfinch.

well as entomologist, commenting on birds in discussion at the meetings and addressing the Society on ornithological topics – 'Flight of birds', 'Bird Life of the Scilly Isles' and 'Migration of Birds', which were published as summaries in the *Proceedings*. These are particularly interesting, since they demonstrate his interest in bird biology and behaviour.

Frohawk did his own taxidermy and some mounted showcases and round skins which he prepared at various stages of his life from 1877 are now in the collections of the Booth Museum, Brighton, Sussex.

Frohawk had a sustained interest in birds and built up considerable knowledge and experience over the years. However, he was very busy with the commissioned

Monochrome water-colour drawing of a swallow.

artwork needed to earn a living as well as with developing his major research project on butterfly life cycles, so he had little time to indulge in bird-watching in the later part of his career. Towards the end of his life in the 1930s, when commissioned work was steadily giving way to his own projects and books, he had an agreement with the publisher Ward Lock to write and illustrate a small popular book on British birds. This was duly done but publication was held up during the war years and the original artwork for many of the plates was destroyed when the publisher's building suffered bomb damage. The book was eventually published posthumously in 1951 under the title *British Birds* after other artists had been called upon to make up the missing plates.

11

Out and About

Contact with the countryside was one of Frohawk's greatest enjoyments, and he always took what opportunities he could to explore the immediate open spaces around his home. He was a strong well-built man, capable of covering many miles in a day's walk and took pride in his fitness. In his memoirs he recalls sessions at the gymnasium at Crystal Palace and working with dumb-bells. In those days before the widespread ownership of motor vehicles, walking was an important way of getting about, particularly in times of economic hardship. We have already seen how he walked from New Cross to Eltham and back visiting his mother in the 1880s. Frohawk enjoyed his own company and often went on long solitary walks, but at other times he was glad to have the companionship of family and friends of similar bent.

THE HOME COUNTIES

From the Croydon area, he would visit West Wickham, Addington, Chipstead and Box Hill. Around Croydon in those days:

> The open country started at Halling Park, south Croydon, when the Brighton Road was a rural roadway with a little row of cottages, a lonely house where an old Hermit lived and the three Public Houses chiefly patronised by travellers from outlying districts . . .
>
> Adjoining [Caterham Junction was] the wild uncultivated Riddlesdown with a rough growth of chalk vegetation and flourishing Juniper bushes. This noted chalk down is now [1940] a residential suburban estate.

And in the same area:

> In the 'seventies' and 'eighties' the Shirley Hills, then usually known as the Addington Hills, were delightfully rural, little frequented, and the haunt of many animals, birds and insects.

Frohawk also explored the countryside further east into north Kent, both when his mother lived at Eltham between 1884 and 1887 and also when staying with the Wood family at Chatham. T.W. Wood was also a naturalist and artist who

*Brimstone butterfly (*Gonepteryx rhamni)*; an unusual variety from Bristol, illustrated in* Varieties of British Butterflies.

*Peacock butterfly (*Inachis io) *bred in captivity. From* Varieties of British Butterflies.

preceded Frohawk as zoological illustrator for *The Field*, but it was his brother John Wood with whom Frohawk often went walking:

> Shortly after the death of T.W. Wood the animal artist, his brother John became one of my greatest friends with whom I stayed many times at his place at Chatham. Being a retired man, he spent much time in exploring the rural parts of Kent, walking 20 or 30 miles in a day, when I had also the pleasure of accompanying him. And how peaceful those country walks were in those happy days of quietude.

Country roads, lanes and waysides were unspoilt by traffic . . . one could walk with peace and comfort, only a gentle trotting horse to take the countryman on his journey, or a farm cart would be the normal vehicle one would meet . . . Now and again we would come to a heap of stones being broken up for mending the turnpike, and would chat with the old stone-breaker with his long-handled hammer. This was long before tarred roads were thought of, the only discomfort was caused by the dust. On dry summer days it was usual for the wayside vegetation to be covered with road dust, hence main roads were to be avoided for the pleasanter lanes and field-paths.

A very memorable walk was on April 22nd 1893 from Headcorn to Tenterden, 9 miles, just before the opening of the railway between these places . . . In Surrey and elsewhere in the south, the fine dry spell started on March 5th, and continued almost unbroken until mid-September. When walking that day with my friend who re-marked 'It is just like a hot August day', he held an open umbrella to keep off the hot suns rays.

On all of these walks, whilst noting the weather and enjoying the views, Frohawk always had an eye open for things of natural history interest:

Frohawk and Valezina collecting butterflies at Denny in the New Forest, Hampshire.

Another memorable walk on the 15.v.1897 was when I saw one of the rarest summer migratory birds to this country viz. a Lesser Grey Shrike, up till that date this was only the fifth example that had been seen in Britain. It is recorded in *The Birds of Kent* by Dr. Norman Ticehurst.

Frohawk also contributed a note on this discovery to *The Field* (published 29 May 1897).

In the first two decades of the twentieth century Frohawk lived mostly in Essex, a place he greatly enjoyed:

> I found south-eastern Essex to be one of the richest places in the country for the British Fauna and Flora that I know of. The varied country consists of woods, rough uncultivated fields, marshes, arable and grazing ground and copses. On the south is the Thames estuary with its mud flats and the river Crouch on the east. The main soil being clay, which I have generally noticed is productive of a great variety of insects and rich in various plants.

He goes on to recall the abundance of wildlife in the garden and meadow of his house 'Uplands' at Thundersley, which included twenty-six species of butterflies, three pairs of nightingales, nightjars, partridges and a barn owl. With the exception of the partridge, these birds are now far less common than they were in Frohawk's time.

SUSSEX

As well as exploring the countryside around his home, holidays provided further opportunity and a greater change of scene. Sometimes the family went to Sussex, where his widow and youngest daughter later settled some years after he died:

> From the autumn of 1932 we spent very delightful holidays both in the spring and autumn until 1939 (when war was proclaimed) at Apple Tree Cottage, Rotherfield, Sussex, a charming cottage belonging to the Butlers . . . A real dream cottage covered with roses and creepers. I found the surrounding country poor as regards butterflies excepting the orange tip which abounds there. The walks are delightful hills and dales, the banks in springtime are teaming with flowers, primroses and violets in profusion and beds of Cuckoo flowers [a food plant of the orange tip caterpillar], stitchworts, campion and wood sorrel. Ferns abound, and wild hyacinths [bluebells] in the woods.

THE NEW FOREST

Whilst Rotherfield was poor in butterflies, the New Forest in Hampshire abounded with them and this was a place to which Frohawk made an almost annual pilgrimage. His name was closely associated with the New Forest from the visits he made in search of butterflies over the best part of a lifetime, and he became known as one of the local characters, 'the old man of the forest'.

My first visit to the New Forest was in July 1888. During the night (18th) a violent thunderstorm with very heavy rain. At 8 a.m. it quite cleared up and was followed by bright sunshine, but at 4 p.m. another thunderstorm broke over the forest. At 8.30 a.m. the forest became like a hot-house everything steaming from the hot sun on the dripping foliage.

I shall never forget the impression it made on my friend J. Wood (brother of T.W. Wood the artist) and self. Insects of all kinds literally swarmed. Butterflies were in profusion, the Silver-washed Fritillary (*Argynnis paphia*) were in hoards in every ride and the beautiful var. *valezina* was met with at every few yards as were both the Dark Green and High Brown Fritillaries, the elegant White Admiral (*Limenitis camilla*) were sailing about in quantity everywhere. On a bank under a sallow was a large female Purple Emperor (*Apatura iris*) with its wings expanded in the sun, evidently washed out of the sallow by rain. The Large Tortoiseshell (*Nymphalis polychloros*) was a frequent occurrence and the Brimstone (*Gonepteryx rhamni*) abundant in every ride.

Frohawk was heavily bitten by the Forest bug:

*Silver-washed fritillary (*Argunnis paphia, form nigrizina) *collected in the New Forest in 1918. From* Varieties.

*High brown fritillary (*Argynnis adippe*); male albino collected in the New Forest in 1918. From* Varieties.

I visited the Forest seven consecutive years after that memorable year, but I found after the middle 'nineties' butterflies decreased in numbers and until 1918 they were notably much scarcer . . .

However, there was an improvement the next year in 1919 when:

We returned from the New Forest after a most enjoyable holiday and

*White Admiral (*Ladoga camilla, form nigrina*) collected in the New Forest in 1919. From* Varieties.

Monochrome water-colour sketch of a New Forest glade rich in butterflies. A painting developed from this is now in the possession of the Rothschild family.

a very successful butterfly collecting experience. All species numerous and varieties abundant.

DORSET

Frohawk also discovered Dorset, another rich area for butterflies:

> In the early 30's Worth Matravers near Swanage was a charming spot not spoilt by any visitors. I found the Wild Cabbage growing freely on the rocky coast. The Purbeck Hills are noted for the wonderful view obtained of the country. One day I counted eight heath fires in the distance. They were disastrous, everything was scorched by the sun July 1921. One day the Purbeck Hills caught fire. At the foot of one steep hill, the flames fanned by a S.W. wind, spread so rapidly that the whole hillside was a roaring sheet of flame. My people being at the top, I signalled for them to make a rapid retreat for safety over the far

152

Frohawk with Valezina and the family dog outside the Square and Compasses, Worth Matravers, Dorset, a county rich in butterflies which Frohawk discovered later in life.

side. In a few minutes the next hill was a mass of torching flames . . . I found the district rich in butterflies.

THE SCILLY ISLES

Further afield, Frohawk made several visits to the Scilly Isles where he took a particular interest in sea birds. He went there with his family in 1897, 1904, 1905, 1907 and 1909, as can be seen by annotations on some of his bird studies. In 1897 they stayed by the lighthouse, and in 1904 their departure from the islands in December was held up by very rough weather during which a large tanker, the *George Wilson*, was wrecked:

> The next day the sea all around the islands was perfectly smooth from the creeping oil from the tanks which covered the surface, the whole area smelling strong of paraffin.

Returning to the Scilly Isles shortly after his second marriage in 1912, he recalls visiting one of the outer western islands and climbing the 120 feet to the summit, where the fissures of the rock 'were tenanted by many razorbills which quite unheeded me, only 3 or 4 ft. away.' The family also enjoyed rambles over the islands.

> The last holiday in these romantic islands we (my wife and daughter) had was in September 1935. One day we spent on Tresco with Major Dorrien-Smith and friends. We looked over his fine collection of birds obtained in the islands, dating back for many years, consisting of several rarities and varieties, one of the last acquired . . . is a fine example of the American Goshawk shot at Tresco Dec. 28 1935. This being only the second authentic occurrence of this bird in this country.

The Dorrien-Smith family still live at Tresco Abbey. Frohawk also related accounts of the plagues of tiger moth caterpillars in the islands during the early part of this century where they fed on any plants they could find, but were in their turn fed upon by cuckoos.

GALLOWAY

During the Second World War Frohawk lived for part of the time in Galloway, and in the list of members published in the *Proceedings of the South London Entomological and Natural History Society* his address for 1940–41 is given as Borgan Cottage, Borgkenman, Newton Stewart, Galloway, situated in the south-western corner of Scotland.

Being over 350 miles north of his home in Surrey, it was not surprising that he found great differences in the landscape and its flora and fauna, and there were plenty of new things to see. By this time he was nearing his 80s, his eyesight was rapidly deteriorating and he had more or less dropped the commissioned artwork for books and magazines. However, Frohawk still took a very lively interest in exploring Galloway, and having more leisure than in his earlier years he was able to diversify his studies and took up botany.

> Galloway is rich with wild flowers that are both prolific and rich in colour. I have found some which I have not noticed in the south. Amongst these is the Butterwort *Pinguicula vulgaris* one of the insect-eating plants. A single handsome purple flower on a stem about 4 inches high, a few ovate succulent light greenish-yellow leaves found on a boggy rocky spot in June. Also on the hills a large wild pansy (*Viola lutea*) of a rich purple and a little yellow. On a rough sea wall at Wigtown, luxuriant in mixed vegetation, I found at the end of June an abundance of Crow Garlic (*Allium vianeale*) the stems if broken smell very strongly of garlic. The growth of Bracken is amazing. It is covering the county, the hills are overgrown with it. The heather has almost completely disappeared, only here and there are purple patches visible. A bad look-out for grouse.

Here we see him looking at the countryside with the eye of the sportsman as well as the naturalist.

> There are no elms in the Bargrennan district, the principal trees are oaks, birch, ash and firs, larch, spruce, pine, also alder, hazel and ancient bushes of blackthorn and whitethorn. Bog myrtle is abundant on all the boggy ground. Bluebell (*Scilla nutans*) abundant, flowers large and rich in colour. In marshy spots at the base of the rocky hills, the water avens (*Geum rivale*) is common in places Aug. 16 I found plants of Grass of Parnassus (*Parnassia palustris*) growing in a boggy spot at Bargrennan. It has been recorded from Ayrshire and Kirkcudbrightshire.

Frohawk knew the red squirrel from his younger days when it lived on Tooting Common and Lloyd Wood, Croydon, in the late nineteenth century, but by 1940 this animal had disappeared from the south to be replaced by the introduced American grey squirrel. In Scotland, where the red squirrel still lives, he was able to renew his acquaintance with this animal.

> The British Red Squirrel is still fairly common in the wooded valleys, the American Grey Squirrel which has caused the disappearance of the form in the south has not reached Scotland. I watched one for many minutes on the ground apparently feeding on the young blades of grass on April 11th with a cream coloured tail and also ear tufts . . . I have never noticed them in the south until July with cream tails

which I believe are only assumed in the summer and distinguishes the British squirrel from the continental species which does not assume the cream coloured tail.

With time to observe, even in his old age Frohawk eagerly followed the season through, clearly excited by the contrasts in the sequence of events between north and south. He records the first willow warbler, swallows, swifts and the butterflies – green-veined white, large skipper, and familiar garden friends such as the small tortoiseshell, peacock and small white. The latter were described as 'busy laying eggs all day on cabbages August 1st' and he evidently did not disturb them. He records woodcocks nesting nearby, but, although he looked, he could see no signs of eagles and remarked on the lack of deer, foxes and badgers which he knew in the south. Tree-creepers nested in an old post close to the cottage.

In mid-June the family went to stay for a week with the Reverend Crossier at Wigtown on the coast, where they enjoyed a fine view across Wigtown Bay.

One of the highlights of the year in Scotland was seeing the Scotch argus butterfly, a northern species that was abundant on boggy ground. This was the subject of a water-colour which Frohawk did as a birthday card to his daughter Valezina, painted when he was eighty years of age. This was published as a cover illustration of *Frederick William Frohawk: A memoir* by his daughter Valezina Bolingbroke (1977).

OTHER TRAVEL

Frohawk always enjoyed exploring new places, but, with the exception of a visit to Amsterdam Zoo, he never went abroad; the two opportunities which he had to join expeditions overseas were turned down as he was about to get married at the time. Natural history illustration was not well paid, and Frohawk had neither the money nor the time to undertake journeys abroad himself, particularly with his family responsibilities which he took seriously. His daughter Valezina recollects that he once went to the zoo in Amsterdam but he does not mention this in his memoir and he was not known to go abroad on any other occasion. Frohawk met many well-travelled naturalists and enjoyed hearing of their exploits and illustrating some of the specimens they had collected. His first-hand experience of live animals from abroad was all obtained at visits to zoos at London, Crystal Palace and Manchester. With such an observant eye and a delight in any new discovery, Frohawk was able to have far more exciting adventures at home compared with many who undertook exotic foreign tours without 'the seeing eye'.

Whilst he savoured being out and about in the countryside, Frohawk's painstaking and time-consuming natural history illustration had to be undertaken indoors in the studio. With very tight publication deadline dates and the need to earn an adequate income to support his family, he had very little free time.

The excursions into the countryside, which kept his inspiration alive, were, for much of his working life, confined to Sundays or to family holidays. Countryside writers like W.H. Hudson and Edward Thomas similarly worked to very tight publishing schedules to support themselves and they too had limited free time to enjoy the country.

Other places which Frohawk visited are evident from the locality data with some of the specimens illustrated in his own books or in annotations to drawings where the place is followed by 'captured F.W.F.' He had evidently collected in Devon and Cornwall, perhaps when on the way to the Scilly Isles and when in search of the large blue butterfly, and various places in Sussex including Harting Combe and Abbots Wood, at Woolmer Forest, Hampshire and at Broadstairs, Kent.

In travelling to different sites Frohawk was limited by the availability of public transport (i.e. trains or buses) and in later years by motor transport provided by friends. In his younger days Frohawk travelled many miles on foot. Although the bicycle came to be a very popular means of independent transport at the turn of the century, they were expensive to buy, and Frohawk never rode one himself. His

Frohawk and Douglas Forsyth Johnstone travelled by motorbike to Hadleigh Woods, Essex, May 1921.

157

Essex friend, Douglas Forsyth Johnstone had a motor cycle and they were both photographed by the motor cycle on a collecting trip to Hadleigh Woods, so it is possible that Frohawk rode as a pillion passenger on this.

In his memoir, Frohawk recalls the different types of vehicle that he had seen in use during his lifetime and which included the velocipede, a wooden bicycle or 'bone-shaker', penny farthing bicycles, the hansom cab, horse-drawn and electric trams and early motor vehicles:

> At the end of the last century, the best made bikes were very expensive costing between £25 and £30. At the beginning of the present century motor cars were a curiosity on the roads, and were hooted at by cab drivers and others. When cars became common on the highways, they raised such volumes of dust, that smothered everything, so much so that houses became vacant from being uninhabitable through the nuisance. This state of affairs continued for some years, resulting in a lengthy correspondence in the press how best to cope with the difficulty, which finally after various trials resulted in tarring the roads.

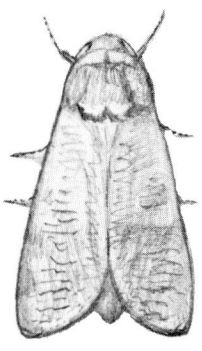

12

Frohawk and his World

A lifetime stretching from 1861 to 1946 witnessed some fundamental changes in the British way of life. Frohawk was brought up in mid-Victorian England when there were large country houses kept in order by vast numbers of servants; women wore long dresses (the crinoline and the bustle); and apart from steam trains, transport relied largely on the horse and, locally, on human foot. By the end of his life, the social structure of Britain had changed: servants were no longer available in the same numbers or under the same conditions and there was a move towards the smaller house. Dress became less formal and more practical, and transport was revolutionised by the internal combustion engine with cars, buses and aircraft becoming part of everyday experience.

Frohawk's own life changed from the affluent country house of his childhood to more modest situations matching his earnings as an illustrator without supplement from private income. Financially he seemed to live fairly close to the wind and there seemed a perpetual pressing need to take on any commissions for work which came along. Creative work is rarely very rewarding in financial terms and does not provide much opportunity to save funds for the future. Frohawk's later years were made a little easier by the Civil List Pension of £100 a year awarded to him in 1932, and increased to £200 a year in 1943.

Frohawk's observations on his world in his notes and his memoir give an extraordinary and vivid insight into these eighty years of dramatic change.

TRANSPORT

In his memoir, Frohawk recalls the advances in transport from the days of horse-drawn vehicles or railways through to the appearance of bicycles, trams and motor vehicles.

> The Hansom Cab invented by J. Hansom in 1843 became the popular vehicle in cities until the introduction of Motor cabs. The old four-wheeled cab, commonly called 'growler', was in use before the Hansom, but the latter with its two wheels and the driver perched up

159

behind became more in vogue, and was speedier, it seated two persons. It is now about 80 years since the first tramway was opened in London, when they were drawn by horses until the middle of the 'eighties' when steam cables were used, then followed electricity. In 1884 I frequently journeyed from New Cross to Blackfriars by tram which used to occupy over an hour, the roof seats were the old-fashioned 'knife-board' type, i.e. a long bench down the centre sitting back-to-back. The tram jogging along at a miserably slow pace, being drawn by three mules each having a jingling bell attached to the harness.

FASHION

There were also great changes in fashions, some of which adversely affected the welfare of wild animals:

It was not until the middle of the 'sixties' that the crinoline finally disappeared. I can just recollect them being worn, in fact my first butterfly net had a crinoline-steel for the rim. Full dresses with many flounces and of Dolly Varden patterns, small straw hats ornamented with plenty of artificial flowers worn on the forehead were considered 'chic' and long handled parasols to match. Then the extreme followed with very tight fitting dresses. The first I noticed in 1875 was a lady of fashion mounting with apparent difficulty a flight of stairs on South-sea pier. These remained fashionable until the early eighties when an extreme transformation scene appeared in the form of the grotesque bustle. This hideous fashion distorting the hinder part of the figure comparable to very bad elephantiasis . . . In the nineties large leg-o-mutton sleeves with great puffed shoulders, like high epaulettes were quite the height of fashion, and large floral trimmed flat hats. The long skirts which were worn must have been most unhygienic sweeping along through all the filth of public highways, the wearers totally disregarding the disgusting custom. It is surprising how fashion overcomes all things.

As a naturalist, Frohawk expressed concern over the use of animal furs in fashions and also the exploitation of tropical birds and their feathers for hat decoration. In 1885 the Selborne Society was set up, and one of its prime objects was to bring an end to the destruction of colourful birds to grace ladies' hats. The Royal Society for the Protection of Birds originated from an informal group set up in 1889.

The fur trade for supplying women's apparel is the cause of gross cruelty in most cases. The trapping of animals for their skins ought to be abolished, it is repulsive to realize what horrible cruelty it causes . . . If it is necessary that furs are to be worn, skins of rabbits and hares would amply suffice as they can be dyed to represent otter, beaver, seal and other animals, and the general public are unable to detect a faked fur from the genuine article.

Birds did receive some protection in the form of an Act of Parliament:

> To abolish the wholesale destruction of humming birds and other bright plumaged birds for millinery purposes, a Plumage Bill prohibiting the sale of bird skins became law. Previously there were annual auction sales in London, when enormous numbers of birds, amounting to many thousands of humming birds, parrots, and others found ready purchasers to decorate womens' hats. The feathers of pheasants and domestic poultry would have supplied all the needs for millinery requirements, and would give equal satisfaction to the goddesses of fashion.

LONDON

London expanded drastically during Frohawk's lifetime, first by the growth of belts of Victorian and Edwardian suburbs and then by the big building phase beyond that during the inter-war years for commuters, made possible by improved public transport:

> It is now seventy years since I first saw London and the suburban districts, and how all parts of the metropolitan area have changed since then, I cannot say for the better . . . In those years not so very far back, many of the surrounding suburbs resembled rural peaceful villages. In Fleet Street, many notables resided in the past, judges and sergeants of law each possessed a dwelling. Near by was Hollywell Street, known as 'Booksellers' Row' where an interesting half-hour might be spent wandering down the Row gazing on the quaint old books where many bargains might sometimes be gleaned.

The Victorians were keen on exhibitions and museums. The Crystal Palace near Croydon always had a range of interesting displays and events which included model dinosaurs, stuffed animals, butterflies and moths, an aquarium, monkey house, art gallery, sculpture, shows of the Kennel Club, poultry, cage birds, pigeons, a gymnasium, firework displays, concerts and pantomimes. Aquaria sprang up in many towns, although few of them remain today. Frohawk recalls one in Westminster:

> There was the very attractive resort, the Aquarium at Westminster where a great variety of shows were always being held, and plenty of attractions. In the 'eighties' J.T. Carrington a well known entomolog-

ist held entomological meetings once a month in the annexe there, this provided members free admission to the aquarium. I first attended a meeting there in 1881, and very interesting it was. Many well known collectors were present. After the meetings, we went 'sight-seeing'.

PEOPLE AND PLACES

Throughout his life Frohawk met many famous and interesting people, some of whom have featured in earlier chapters. Sportsmen and big game hunters were very much part of late Victorian society:

> Among the famous men I have intimately known, was the renowned F.C. Selous, the great Big-game hunter of Africa, for many reasons his name is outstanding in bravery and endurance. He was a man (like many others of notoriety) of modesty, a non-exaggerator and of strict truthfulness. He only conversed on his exploits to those he knew intimately and would be interested . . . Altogether he spent twenty years after big game . . . He said for a rest and change from hunting big game he would spend a day or two collecting some of the wonderful and beautiful butterflies, some being new species, now in the British Museum. I spent several days with him at his place at Worplestone, Surrey where he had a museum containing a fine collection of trophies collected by himself.

Frohawk also knew the falconer F.H. Salvin:

> From the end of 1888 for many years I frequently visited the Wilsons at their fine place 'Heatherbank', Weybridge Heath and stayed there at times for two or three days. My friend Scott B. Wilson and I often went from there to spend the day with Capt. F.H. Salvin, the renowned falconer. On his lawn he usually kept a few trained hawks perched on bow perches. He also had his tame otters and cormorants. I often gave the otters dainty bits in the way of any large beetles, cockroaches, much to their pleasure . . . The Capt. told me it takes $12\frac{1}{2}$ lbs of fish daily to keep a cormorant in health.

Frohawk was familiar with Wisley in Surrey, in its early days as a private residence before it was taken over by the Royal Horticultural Society in 1904:

> Mr. A.F. Wilson was the owner of the well known delightful semi-wild experimental gardens at Wisley, near Weybridge, where we often spent many pleasant hours . . . Wilson was the first to produce the *blue* primrose, now so commonly grown in gardens. He showed me some of the original plants the flowers of which were of a rich pure

cobalt-blue . . . When he passed away his son Scott told me that he sold the gardens for £11,000 to Hanbury who gave the estate to the Botanical Society. A fortnight after my first marriage in June 1895 my wife and self attended a well-to-do garden party held in the Wisley gardens. We there made acquaintance with some well known prominent people among whom were art critics, authors and nobility.

Frohawk also met John Hancock, a naturalist well known in malacological circles as a co-author of a classic work on seaslugs, *A monograph of the British Nudibranchiate Mollusca* (Alder and Hancock, 1845–55).

A few of Frohawk's paintings went to the United States:

> In 1933 I met Dr. Casey Wood of Philadelphia by appointment. He was anxious to make a selection of two or three samples of my paintings of birds etc. to hang in the picture gallery at Philadelphia, amongst the work of other European artists and was pleased with those he selected.

THE SKY AND THE WEATHER

Frohawk's interest in the sky as an artist and as a countryman extended to astronomical phenomena, some of which he sketched and painted. During his lifetime he saw some fine comets, including Halley's Comet in 1910 which returned in 1985–6:

> I remember an outstanding comet was that of 1882, it was such a striking spectacle in the S. eastern sky on Nov. 4th at 4 a.m. the sky being cloudless, that I made a pencil sketch of the object. In the evenings of May 1910 about sunset the wonderful Halley's comet was a beautiful ornament in the midsummer evening sky, this I also sketched as seen just above the western horizon at Rayleigh Essex. The press indulged in the various superstitious correspondence from the ignorant public as it was predicted that the comet would collide with this planet resulting in the end of the world.

In 1910 there was another good comet to be seen:

> The new Twilight Comet at Rayleigh, Essex on January 21st at 5.20 p.m. 1910, only four days after it was discovered at Johannesburg. I had a remarkably good view of the new comet, the sky being very clear at the time, it was plainly visible to the naked eye and presented quite a conspicuous object. I made a sketch of it on the spot. The tail swept upwards in a slight curve directed towards the planet Venus which it rivalled in brilliancy.

Pencil drawing of the Twilight Comet of 1910, as seen from Rayleigh, Essex, at 5.20 pm.

Another phenomenon he experienced was the volcanic eruption on the Indonesian island of Krakatoa that had effects throughout the world:

> In August 1883 occurred the great eruption of Krakatoa which was so violent that it filled the air of a great portion of the world with volcanic dust that was estimated to be shot up to enormous heights, one estimate as much as 17 miles, and the finest particles remained

suspended in the atmosphere which produced the most wonderful sunsets during the following autumn and early winter seen in this country. I remember they became so spectacular that many people congregated in the evenings on the parade in front of the Crystal Palace 400 ft. elevation giving a fine view of the brilliant sunsets, one I sketched in oils on Nov, 27 1883.

As a naturalist Frohawk was well aware of the importance of weather in bringing about changes in the cycles of natural populations. The butterflies in each season were clearly affected by weather, and the birds too. But he also took an interest in weather for its own sake and, unlike many people, seemed to enjoy thunder storms:

A great thunderstorm is one of nature's awe inspiring and majestic phenomena, it commands both earth and sky by its mighty force and magnitude, generally accompanied by the savagery of all the elements lashed into one tremendous uproar . . . The most severe thunderstorms I can recall to mind during the past seventy years were those of 1874, 1897, 1924. How vividly I remember Whit Monday of 1874. The day opened with a fine warm summer morning, therefore my brother and I decided to have a day's butterfly collecting on the Surrey Hills, so we tramped off from West Croydon to Riddlesdown, arriving at the ground by what was then a little country station known as Caterham Junction (now a big suburban station) amidst the wild and peaceful surroundings. Being a Bank Holiday there were a few people about. During the hour before noon, every now and then we heard in the south distant rumblings and thought it might be a big gunfire at Portsmouth, but soon after midday big dark clouds swept up from the S.W. and the atmosphere became oppressive and hot. Then suddenly a violent storm broke with a lashing rain, dazzling flashes of lightning and tremendous explosions of thunder which caused us to make all speed to the nearest shelter, the railway-arch where we found a number of holiday makers sheltering and evidently alarmed by the fierceness of the storm which was terrific . . . Many of the flashes of lightning hissed as they passed through the archway, it is a great wonder no-one taking shelter there was struck down. This terrific storm continued with all its violence until 4 p.m. The downpour of rain was so dense that the limitation of vision was reduced to about 50 yds. The lower parts of the country were flooded. As we trudged homeward we passed a pair of bus horses lying dead struck by lightning, also several sheep dead in a meadow . . . I was then only eleven years of age but the magnitude of the tempest has always remained so vividly in my mind.

Another storm which he remembered was many years later, again whilst out on field work:

The most severe storm probably ever experienced in Britain, was that of July 4th 1924. I had been out butterfly collecting at Goodwood with Baron Bouck, about 4.30 p.m. we heard distant thunder in the south. Increasing in intensity it broke over the whole of the southern counties about 6 p.m. when the rain started. The tempest was too severe for me to journey from South Godstone, Surrey to Beckenham, Kent, so was forced to stay there for the memorable night and what a night it was, all the evening the lightning was becoming more frequent and during the whole night the lightning was so continuous that the rooms were lighted by the flashes as if lighted by means of artificial electricity. At 4 a.m. an appalling explosion occurred as if the whole house was struck, instead a large beech tree a few yds away from the house was shattered. This terrible storm raged from 6 p.m. until 6 a.m.

During his long life, Frohawk saw many extremes of weather:

As regards the weather during my lifetime, I mainly associate with entomology therefore I will allude to outstanding years as I remember them . . . We commonly hear the remark 'old fashioned winter' alluding to severity of the weather, and it is generally supposed that the seasons have altered from those of long past years. But as a matter of fact, the records dating back for centuries prove the seasons were similar then, some, perhaps a series of three or four very severe winters were followed by others of exceptional mildness, as was the case in 1878–9, 1879–80, 1880–1, three winters of great severity, then followed a series of mild ones. For the past half century I have carefully observed the conditions of the weather prevailing through the year, and long ago came to the conclusion that it is invariably finer during the first half of the moon than later, also when the moon is about full the days are cloudy and dull, but the nights are brilliantly fine, as the moon rises the clouds disperse. I have noticed this for 58 years ever since a long walk of 42 miles on the brilliantly lit night on September 15th 1883, when the moon was at its fullest. I have also noted that after the first week of July the weather becomes unsettled and many dull days follow with much rain, and the last ten days of the month are generally cold and dull.

He recalls some years which were exceptions, with fine Julys in 1881, 1893 and 1921, the last two being associated with long periods of drought. Severe winters are also discussed:

Very rarely snow falls on Christmas Day. I can only recall a few times when it has been snowy on that day . . . It was in the severe winter of 1874, just about Christmas, that the whole of the Brighton district was frozen up, as I remember walking from Brighton to Hove, a rough

Eclipse of the sun from Upper Norwood on 28 May 1900 at 3.49 pm.

icy roadway by the edge of fields . . . bordered by rough snow covered banks on which a great number of half frozen birds had resorted. Many were bramblings, redwings, fieldfares, chaffinches, yellow-hammers and others, but what struck me most were the quantities of bramblings. I may add that Hove then was quite distinct from Brighton, it consisted, if I remember rightly, of coast-guards' cottages and a rather large frozen pool, with waders round the edge, a shore-shooter stalking them. I don't think there were any houses then to the west of the Brighton pier . . . But the winter of 1895 was one of the severest and longest on record . . . The Thames was frozen over all along the London area. It was the first appearance of seagulls on the river as far up as London, a few being driven up for food, each successive winter the number increased.

When snow falls either in spring when the leaves are coming out on the trees or in autumn before they have fallen, the great weight of snow accumulating on the leaves can cause spectacular damage:

A similar heavy fall of snow took place in the early autumn of 1883 when the oaks and elms were still thick of foliage. I remember taking a long walk to view the damage done in the Surrey woodlands. Great trees were split, huge limbs were torn off and strewn about as if a fierce hurricane had swept the country.

167

The wooden cross on Frohawk's grave at Headley, Surrey, with a carving of the Camberwell beauty.

For the last six years of his life, Frohawk's sight did not allow him to do much drawing or close work and he had no major projects on hand, although he was able to enjoy his year in Galloway, Scotland, to the full with an enthusiasm unabated by advancing years. He survived the Second World War and was able

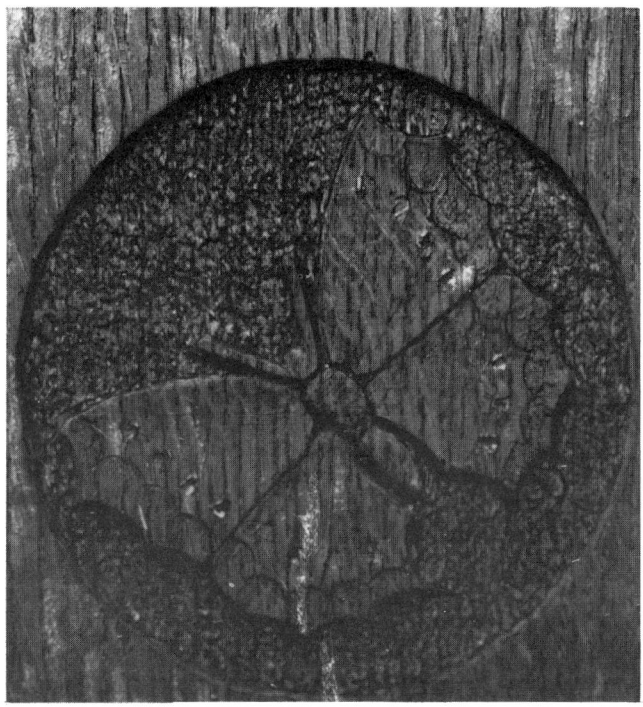

A close-up of the carving.

to meet his many entomological friends and followers at the annual exhibition of the South London Entomological and Natural History Society just a few months before he died. F.W. Frohawk's life ended on 10 December 1946 at his home in Sutton, Surrey, where he had lived since 1927. He was buried at Headley in Surrey, an area which is still open country, and on his grave is a wooden cross with the carving of a Camberwell beauty butterfly. His better known memorials are his books and illustrations in libraries throughout the world.

13

Frohawk – A Measure of his Life

Frohawk's consuming interest in natural history and drawing, with its very early beginnings, provided the backbone of his life. He was always busy studying natural history or illustrating and spent very long hours initially developing these skills and later producing work in order to earn a living and support his family. It is often said that it is a mistake to turn a hobby into a career, but Frohawk would have done things no other way and he continued to enjoy these interests to the full even though he earned his living by them.

Frohawk was very single-minded and showed an extraordinary amount of self-discipline when working at home; his sheer stamina is astounding for he was able to produce good quality and accurate illustrations even when drawing late at night after a full and tiring day of similar work at the Natural History Museum. He clearly had a natural aptitude for drawing, but looking at his early pencil sketches at the Zoo from 1880 onwards, it is evident how much he improved through constant practice and the development of new techniques.

Throughout his life Frohawk worked under pressure, and were all his drawings, paintings and writings to be gathered together the enormous volume of work would be astounding, even allowing for sixty years or so as a professional illustrator. Although in his youth he had ample time to potter about, exploring the countryside, in later years, and especially after his marriage, such self-indulgent pursuits had to be sacrificed to the programme of paid work in the studio. Any days out Frohawk had, and even family holidays, were invariably collecting trips for the research project of that particular time.

Valezina, Frohawk's youngest daughter, recalls that family and friends were all convinced that Frohawk would never have achieved so much without the support of his second wife Mabel. She devoted her whole life to him, being fully prepared to let natural history and artwork come first at all times and sheltering him from tedious day to day domestic matters in the running of house and family.

Many amateur artists are prone to overwork a painting with a consequent loss of spontaneity, tonal variation and clarity. The fast rate at which Frohawk worked for commissioned illustrations may well have been advantageous in preventing this happening in his drawings. Whilst doing the bird pictures for A.G. Butler's book *British Birds with their Nests and Eggs*, Frohawk achieved a rate of four paintings a week. These were complete pictures with a background as well as the bird.

Books are normally indexed under the name of the author who provides the written text and artists are often given limited recognition on the title page and may not necessarily be included in library catalogue cards except in specialist libraries. Although the signature of the artist may appear in the illustration, a special effort has to be made to look for it. Many people earlier in the twentieth century may therefore have been familiar with Frohawk's work without knowing his name or anything about him. However, recognised or not, artists are very important in the book world for, as many modern publishers are fast to realise, pictures can sell a book.

Whilst the illustrations for *The Field* and the Natural History Museum post-cards would have reached a wide audience, many of the books which Frohawk illustrated were at the upper end of the market – fine illustrated books that would have had a limited print run, and by their price reached only a favoured few. Most of the books with chromolithographs fall into this category. Even his butterfly books, for which he is generally remembered in the entomological world, would be found on the bookshelves of only a limited number of entomologists.

Frohawk was over eighty when he died in 1946 and very few people remain who can remember him as a person. His daughter Valezina remembers him as a quiet and highly sensitive person, who had a subtle sense of humour and was a great tease to children. Like most naturalists he was not interested in smart clothes, but preferred comfortable old ones and tended to create his own fashion rather than follow the trend of the time. In entomological work he was much esteemed and liked by almost everyone. However, he was at times the subject of a certain amount of professional jealousy and there were some who went to great pains to criticise his notes in the next issue of the particular journal. This was alluded to in his obituary by Dr Riley in *The Entomologist*.

Throughout his career, and particularly in more difficult times, Frohawk was much indebted to various naturalists like the Hon. Walter (later Lord) Rothschild of Tring and Lord Walsingham who acted as patrons by placing large orders for commissioned work when Frohawk needed them most. In one instance, after the collapse of the Brighton zoo project, it was Lord Walsingham who immediately came to the rescue with an order for 1,000 coloured drawings of microlepidoptera. The first butterfly book was sponsored by Lord Rothschild, who almost certainly helped him financially in many other ways, including his offer to purchase Frohawk's butterfly collection which enabled him to buy his own home. Without Lord Rothschild's help, some things in life which Frohawk and his family enjoyed would not have been possible. The Essex shoot may also have been acquired through some kindly sponsor, and a number of friends lent him cottages for the family holiday, like that of the Butler family at Rotherfield in Sussex. Without these offers of help there would have been fewer extras in life, as one of the problems of freelance work is the irregular and unpredictable flow of cash.

Frohawk and Valezina out collecting butterflies at Harting Combe.

As well as being fortunate enough to enjoy the hospitality and patronage of wealthy naturalists of private means, sometimes working on collections in their fine country estates, Frohawk also received substantial commissions to illustrate the writings of professional zoologists at the British Museum (Natural History); people like Dr A. Gunther and Dr A.G. Butler. Museum work helped to see him through his first winter after the family's financial crisis of 1884. Frohawk was, however, very philosophical about forgoing things which could not be afforded and gained great pleasure and contentment from simple things in life.

In a century of illustrated books Frohawk was not the only bird artist, and in some of the books to which he contributed there are pictures by other artists, particularly Grönvold, Keulemans and Smit. Besides being a bird artist Frohawk was also a good field ornithologist, a national authority on British butterflies and author of both scientific monographs and papers as well as more popular articles in *The Field*. Few people have attempted the research, illustration and text on such a range of zoological subject matter and projects of such long duration.

Frohawk's name was well known in natural history circles of the late nineteenth century and the first half of the twentieth century. He was very much at the centre of things and walked along most interesting corridors of life, meeting other important naturalists and explorers of the world.

Frohawk had an open mind and took an interest in everything. This attitude is apparent in his memoir which covers such a wide spectrum of subjects outside natural history. This eager approach to life retains the fresh curiosity of the mind of the child, and throughout life Frohawk was always keen to extend his knowledge. Towards the end of his life, whilst living for a year in Galloway, Scotland, he took the opportunity of the leisure it afforded to do some field botany. Although he had a good knowledge of plants as a general naturalist, his earlier life and work did not allow time for the study of botany other than studies of plants as food or shelter for butterflies and their caterpillars. In Galloway he also made some water-colour paintings of the plants he found.

In this portrait of F.W. Frohawk, naturalist, artist and author, we can only cover a brief outline of his life and work and introduce his world to the present-day naturalist. The book is in no way definitive and there is much still to be researched on many aspects of his life, development as an artist and achievements in natural history. Only a complete bibliography of his many scattered illustrations, published notes and books could give a true picture of the extent of the vast output by this one man over a period of sixty years at the centre of the British natural history scene at the turn of the century. His many entomological notes, merit further consideration against the modern background of ecology and conservation: his writings hold much information that is of practical use in helping to save some of our rarer butterflies. Indeed, his friend, the Hon. Charles Rothschild, the subject of a recent article in *Natural World* by his daughter Miriam, was a pioneer conservationist far ahead of his time, and Frohawk was likely to have been involved in his early ideas for nature reserves.

Frohawk's work has been neglected in the forty years since his death, particularly as biology has become more scientific with an emphasis on physiology and biochemistry, moving away from descriptive natural history. However, the current movement in ecology, conservation and biological recording of the environment is starting to redress the balance and the detailed work of earlier Victorian naturalists with a broad knowledge of natural history is receiving attention once more. There has also been a revival of interest in the lives of earlier naturalists and their achievements, largely through the work of the Society for the History of Natural History, which is also reflected in the illustrated books published for the layman in recent years. Frohawk had a broad interest in animal life, foreign as well as British. His whole life was a learning process and he never lost his respect and sense of wonder for the natural world: we have much to learn from him.

References

The following reference sources were used in the preparation of this book. Those containing illustrations by F.W. Frohawk are marked with an asterisk (many of his drawings are in the publications of other authors).

The list of publications by Frohawk includes his books, but only a small proportion of the large number of notes and papers written principally for *The Field* and *The Entomologist* over a sixty-year period. In the time available it was not possible to compile a complete bibliography of his published writings and illustrations, but it is hoped that the list presented will provide access to a good selection of his work.

* ADKIN, R., 1897. Varieties of *Abraxas grossulariata*. *The Entomologist 30*, 25.

ALLEN, D.E., 1976. *The Naturalist in Britain*. A social history. Allen Lane, London.

* ALPHERAKY, S., 1905. *The Geese of Europe and Asia*. Rowland Ward, London.

ANON, 1890. The Secretary on additions to the menagerie. *Proceedings of the Zoological Society of London 1890*, 147 (plate XV).

ANON, 1932. The Entomological Club. *The Entomologist 65*, 119–120.

ANON, 1947. Obituary Frederick William Frohawk. *Transactions of the Suffolk Naturalists' Society 6*, lxiv.

ANON, 1952. *Who was Who 1941–50*. Adam and Charles Black, London.

* BARTLETT, E., 1888–89. *A Monograph of the Weaver-birds (Ploceidae), and Arboreal and Terrestrial Finches (Fringillidae)*. Published by the author, Maidstone, Kent.

BLAIR, K.G., 1922–23. Will-o-the-wisp. *Proceedings of the South London Entomological and Natural History Society 1922–23*, 12–29.

* BOLINGBROKE, V., 1977. *Frederick William Frohawk*. E.M. Classey Ltd., Faringdon, Oxon.

* BOULENGER, G.A., 1886. Description of a new iguanoid lizard living in the Society's gardens. *Proceedings of the Zoological Society of London 1886*, 241.

* BOULENGER, G.A., 1886. Remarks on specimens of *Rana arvalis* exhibited in the Society's menagerie. *Proceedings of the Zoological Society of London 1886*, 242–243.

* BOULENGER, G.A., 1886. First report on additions to the Batrachian collection in the Natural History Museum. *Proceedings of the Zoological Society of London 1886*, 411–416.

* BOULENGER, G.A., 1886. On the European species of *Bombinator*. *Proceedings of the Zoological Society of London. 1886*, 499–501.

BRIDSON, R.H., 1978. *The Natterjack Toad*. Nature Conservancy Council, London.

* BUTLER, A.G., 1877–89. *Illustrations of Typical Specimens of Lepidoptera, Heterocera in the Collections of the British Museum*. British Museum (Natural History), London.

* BUTLER, A.G., 1893. On two collections of Lepidoptera sent by H.H. Johnston, Esq., CB from British Central Africa. *Proceedings of the Zoological Society of London 1893*, 642–684.

* BUTLER, A.G., 1894–96. *Foreign Finches in Captivity.* L. Reeve and Co., London.
* BUTLER, A.G., 1895. On collections of Lepidoptera from British Central Africa and Lake Tanganyika. *Proceedings of the Zoological Society of London 1895,* 250–270.
* BUTLER, A.G., 1895. On a small collection of butterflies sent by Mr. Richard Crawshay from the country west of Lake Nyasa. *Proceedings of the Zoological Society of London 1895,* 627–634.
* BUTLER, A.G., 1895. On a small collection of butterflies made by Consul Alfred Sharpe at Zomba, British Central Africa. *Proceedings of the Zoological Society of London 1895,* 720–721.
* BUTLER, A.G., 1895. On Lepidoptera recently collected in British East Africa by Mr. G.F. Scott Elliot. *Proceedings of the Zoological Society of London 1895,* 722–742.
* BUTLER, A.G., 1896–98. *British Birds with their Nests and Eggs.* 6 vols. Brumby and Clarke, London.
* BUTLER, A.G., n.d. (c. 1896–98). *Birds of Great Britain and Ireland.* Caxton Publishing Co., London.
* BUTLER, A.G., 1900. A revision of the butterflies of the genus *Zizera* represented in the collection of the British Museum. *Proceedings of the Zoological Society of London 1900,* 104–111.
* BUTLER, A.G., 1904. *Birds Eggs of the British Isles.* Brumby and Clarke, London.
* CARRINGTON, J.T., 1891. Winged parasite of birds (*Ornithomya avicularia*). *The Field 78,* 574.
CHAPMAN, T.A., 1915. What the larva of *Lycaena arion* does during its last instar. *Transactions of the Entomological Society of London 48,* 291–297.
CHAPMAN, T.A., 1915. Observations completing an outline of the life history of *Lycaena arion,* L. *Transactions of the Entomological Society of London 48,* 298–312.
CHAPMAN, T.A., 1916. The evolution of the habits of the larva of *Lycaena arion,* L. *Transactions of the Entomological Society of London 49,* 315–321.
COLEMAN, W.S., 1860. *British Butterflies.* Routledge, Warne and Routledge, London.
COOKE, W., 1970. *Edward Thomas – a Critical Biography.* Faber, London.
* DRUCE, H. and WALSINGHAM. Th. de Grey, 1881–1915. *Lepidoptera – Heterocera Biologia Centrali Americana, Zool.* Porter and Dulau, London.
* *ENCYCLOPAEDIA BRITANNICA,* 1875–1889. Adam and Charles Black, Edinburgh.
FITTER, R.S.R., 1945. *London's Natural History.* The New Naturalist, Collins, London.
FROHAWK, F.W., 1882. Variety of *Smerinthus tiliae. The Entomologist 15,* 130.
FROHAWK, F.W., 1882. Late stay of swallows and martins. *The Field 60,* 741.
FROHAWK, F.W., 1886. Snipe in a London suburb. *The Field 67,* 84.
FROHAWK, F.W., 1887. Clothes moth larvae. *The Field 70,* 321.
FROHAWK, F.W., 1887. Pellets ejected by birds. *The Field 70,* 778.
FROHAWK, F.W., 1887. Notes on the past entomological season. *The Field 70,* 828.
FROHAWK, F.W., 1888. *Vanessa antiopa* in Kent. *The Field 72,* 316.
FROHAWK, F.W., 1890. Lepidoptera in 1889 – New Forest. *The Entomologist 23,* 68.
FROHAWK, F.W., 1891. Martins and wasps nests. *The Field 78,* 508.
FROHAWK, F.W., 1891. Feeding of lions. *The Field 78,* 509.
FROHAWK, F.W., 1892. Description of a new species of rail from Laysan Island (North Pacific). *Annals and Magazine of Natural History* series 6, *9,* 247–249.
FROHAWK, F.W., 1894. A list of birds observed at Tooting Beck Common, near London. *The Zoologist* 3rd series, *18,* 178–179.

FROHAWK, F.W., 1895. Thrush and hedge sparrow singing during frost. *The Field 85*, 225.

FROHAWK, F.W., 1895. Life history of *Nyssia lapponaria*. *The Entomologist 28*, 237–240.

FROHAWK, F.W., 1895. Productiveness of *Colias edusa*. *The Entomologist 28*, 263.

FROHAWK, F.W., 1897. Lesser Grey Shrike in Kent. *The Field 89*, 839.

FROHAWK, F.W., 1897. Lesser Grey Shrike (*Lanius minor*) in Kent. *The Zoologist* series 4, *1*, 427–428.

FROHAWK, F.W., 1898. Speed of birds. *The Field 92*, 182, 274, 364.

FROHAWK, F.W., 1900. Little Gull (*Larus minutus*) on the Thames. *The Zoologist* series 4, *4*, 83.

FROHAWK, F.W., 1906. Life history of *Aparia crataegi*. *The Entomologist 39*, 132–138.

* FROHAWK, F.W., 1906. Completion of the life-history of *Lycaena arion*. *The Entomologist 39*, 145–147.

FROHAWK, F.W., 1906. Life-history of *Pieris daplidice*. *The Entomologist 39*, 193–196.

FROHAWK, F.W., 1908. Colour variety in the redwing. *The Field 111*, 108.

FROHAWK, F.W., 1908. Wryneck calling in July. *The Field 112*, 104.

FROHAWK, F.W., 1908. Corn bunting singing in October. *The Field 112*, 721.

FROHAWK, F.W., 1908. Habits of the Manx shearwaters. *The Field 112*, 1021.

FROHAWK, F.W., 1912. Varieties of the mole. *The Field 119*, 48.

FROHAWK, F.W., 1912. Food of the great spotted woodpecker. *The Field 119*, 744.

FROHAWK, F.W., 1912. Hibernation of the brimstone butterfly. *The Field 119*, 889.

FROHAWK, F.W., 1912. The drinking habits of butterflies. *The Field 119*, 940.

FROHAWK, F.W., 1912. The large blue butterfly, its history and mystery. *The Field 120*, 1121.

FROHAWK, F.W., 1912. Non-hibernation of the red admiral in Britain. *The Field 119*, 1219.

FROHAWK, F.W., 1913. Variation in colour in birds and insects. *The Field 121*, 434.

FROHAWK, F.W., 1913. Food of the waxwing. *The Field 121*, 590.

FROHAWK, F.W., 1913. Immigration of the clouded yellow. *The Field 122*, 118.

FROHAWK, F.W., 1913. Grouse feeding upon insects. *The Field 122*, 1147.

FROHAWK, F.W., 1913. Cormorants mode of progress under water. *The Field 122*, 1202.

FROHAWK, F.W., 1914. The holly blue butterfly. *The Field 123*, 936.

FROHAWK, F.W., 1914. Occurrence of the Camberwell beauty. *The Field 124*, 429.

FROHAWK, F.W., 1914. The Camberwell beauty. *The Field 124*, 502.

FROHAWK, F.W., 1914. Great flight of martins. *The Field 124*, 613.

* FROHAWK, F.W., 1914. The smaller British owls. 1. The little owl. *The Field 124*.

* FROHAWK, F.W., 1914. The smaller British owls. 2. Tengmalm's owl. *The Field 124*, 894.

* FROHAWK, F.W., 1914. The smaller British owls. 3. The Scops owl. *The Field 124*, 938.

* FROHAWK, F.W., 1914–1915. A natural history of British butterflies. *The Field 124*, 1060; *125*, 40–41, 77–78, 92–94, 164–165, 208–209, 220–221, 296–297, 340–341, 382–383, 428–429, 474–475, 516–517, 532–533, 573–574, 618–619, 690–691, 704–705, 776–777, 794–795, 869–870, 916–917, 957–958, 996–997, 1042–1043, 1080–1081, 1096–1097; *126*, 42–43, 81–82, 128–129, 178–179, 222–223, 270–271, 312–313, 346–347, 365–366.

* FROHAWK, F.W., 1915. Further observations on the last stage of the larva of *Lycaena*

arion. Transactions of the Entomological Society of London 48, 313–316.

* FROHAWK, F.W., 1915–1916. The 'bird-life of the Scilly Isles. The Manx shearwater'. *Proceedings of the South London Entomological and Natural History Society 1915–1916*, 70–72.

FROHAWK, F.W., 1916. A remarkable variety of the stoat. *The Field 124*, 581.

* FROHAWK, F.W., 1916. Development of the orang-utan. *The Field 127*, 748.

FROHAWK, F.W., 1916. A barred variety of the rook. *The Field 128*, 272.

FROHAWK, F.W., 1916. An unusual nesting site of blackbird. *The Field 128*, 372.

FROHAWK, F.W., 1916. Varieties of the curlew and lapwing. *The Field 128*, 407.

FROHAWK, F.W., 1916. Smooth snakes in the New Forest. *The Field 128*, 714.

FROHAWK, F.W., 1916. Varieties of the red grouse. *The Field 128*, 761.

FROHAWK, F.W., 1916. Varieties of the woodcock. *The Field 128*, 837.

FROHAWK, F.W., 1916. Unusual number of eggs of the song thrush. *The Field 128*, 904.

* FROHAWK, F.W., 1916–1917. Flight of birds. *Proceedings of the South London Entomological and Natural History Society, 1916–1917*, 53–55.

FROHAWK, F.W., 1918. Pigmy shrew in Kent and Essex. *The Field 131*, 30.

* FROHAWK, F.W., 1918. A remarkable homing pigeon. *The Field 131*, 183.

* FROHAWK, F.W., 1918. 'Marvellously quick'. *The Field* 131, 242.

* FROHAWK, F.W., 1918. Illustrations of rabbit traps and snares and cutting the skin preliminary to paunching a rabbit. *The Field 131*, 304, 316, 372, 412, 522.

FROHAWK, F.W., 1918. Abundance of hibernated butterflies. *The Field 131*, 491.

FROHAWK, F.W., 1918. Intelligence of the orang-utan. *The Field 132*, 603.

* FROHAWK, F.W., 1918. *Novitates Zoologicae 25*, Plate 8.

* FROHAWK, F.W., 1919. *Birds Beneficial to Agriculture*. British Museum (Natural History), London.

FROHAWK, F.W., 1919. Butterflies imbibing their excretion. *The Field 134*, 291.

FROHAWK, F.W., 1919. Unequal number of sexes in butterflies. *The Field 134*, 603.

FROHAWK, F.W., 1920. Unusual immigration of red admirals and painted ladies. *The Field 135*, 794.

* FROHAWK, F.W., n.d. (1924). *Natural History of British Butterflies*. 2 vols. Hutchinson, London.

FROHAWK, F.W., 1924. Unusual abundance of *Pyrameis atalanta*. The Entomologist 57, 257.

FROHAWK, F.W., 1924. The black redstart in England. *The Field 143*, 430.

FROHAWK, F.W., 1924. Variation of the red-legged and common partridge. *The Field 143*, 556.

FROHAWK, F.W., 1924. Colour changes in the stoat. *The Field 143*, 636.

FROHAWK, F.W., 1924. The red admiral in June. *The Field 144*, 83.

FROHAWK, F.W., 1924. Fieldfare in August. *The Field 144*, 402.

FROHAWK, F.W., 1924. Scarcity of house martins. *The Field 144*, 462.

FROHAWK, F.W., 1924. The Californian quail. *The Field 144*, 712.

FROHAWK, F.W., 1925. The scarcity and disappearance of butterflies. *The Entomologist 58*, 145–147.

FROHAWK, F.W., 1925. Remarkable scarcity of butterflies in the New Forest. *The Entomologist 58*, 250.

FROHAWK, F.W., 1925. *Argynnis paphia* in London suburbs. *The Entomologist 58*, 270.

FROHAWK, F.W., 1926. Clouded yellow in Dorset. *The Field, 148*, 344.

FROHAWK, F.W., 1926. Food of the herring gull. *The Field 148*, 111.

FROHAWK, F.W., 1926. Repeated occurrence of the Apollo butterfly in Britain. *The Field, 148,* 543.

FROHAWK, F.W., 1926. Perseverance of a toad. *The Field 148,* 543.

FROHAWK, F.W., 1926. The scarce swallow-tail. *The Field 148,* 1045.

* FROHAWK, F.W., 1930. Two-horned larvae of *Sphinx ligustri. The Entomologist 63,* 39.

FROHAWK, F.W., 1930. Remarkable vitality of *Cucullia verbasci* pupa. *The Entomologist 63,* 58.

FROHAWK, F.W., 1932. Obituary – D.C. Johnstone, *The Entomologist 65,* 120.

* FROHAWK, F.W., 1934. *The Complete Book of British Butterflies.* Ward Lock and Co., London.

* FROHAWK, F.W., 1938. *Varieties of British Butterflies.* Ward Lock and Co., London.

FROHAWK, F.W., 1945. *Argynnis lathonia* at Sutton. *The Entomologist 78,* 21.

FROHAWK, F.W., 1945. Some natural history problems. *The Field 185,* 223.

* FROHAWK, F.W., 1951. *British Birds.* Ward Lock and Co., London.

FROHAWK, M., 1897. Great grey shrike at Oxted. *The Field 89,* 243.

FROHAWK, M., 1900. Early appearance of *Pieris rapae. The Entomologist 33,* 130.

* GARBOWSKI, T.H., 1895. Aberrations in the structure of appendages in the Coleoptera. *The Entomologist 28,* 125–127.

GARRARD, A.C., 1922. *The Worst Journey in the World.* Constable, London, and also published by the author.

GILBERT, P., 1977. *A Compendium of the Biographical Literature on Deceased Entomologists.* British Museum (Natural History), London.

GREENWAY, J., 1958. *Extinct and Vanishing Birds of the World.* American Committee for International Wildlife Protection. New York, 231–235.

HALL, W.J., 1947. The President's Address. *Proceedings of the Royal Entomological Society of London (C) 11,* 59–60.

HARTERT, E.J.O. and BONHOTE, J.L., 1907. *Proceedings of the Fourth International Ornithological Congress.* Dulau and Co., London.

* JACKSON, C.E., 1975. *Bird Illustrators: Some Artists in Early Lithography.* H.F. and G. Witherby Ltd, London.

JACKSON, F.G., 1899. *A Thousand Days in the Arctic.* Harper and Brothers, London and New York.

JACKSON, R.A., 1947, F.W. Frohawk (1861–1947) [*sic*]. *Proceedings and Transactions of the South London Entomological and Natural History Society 1946–1947,* 5.

JOHNSTONE, J.F., 1912. Duke of Burgundy fritillary. *The Field 119,* 1171.

* JORDAN, K., 1894. New species of Coleoptera from the Indo- and Austro-Malayan region, collected by William Doherty. *Novitates Zoologicae 1,* 104–266.

KENT, W. SAVILLE, 1895. Observations on the frilled lizard *Chlamydosaurus kingi Proceedings of the Zoological Society of London 1895,* 712–719.

* LEECH, J.H., 1889. On the Lepidoptera of Japan and Corea. *Proceedings of the Zoological Society of London 1889,* 474–571.

* LYDEKKER, R., 1893–1896. *The Royal Natural History.* Warne, London.

* LYDEKKER, R., 1899. *The Great and Small Game of Africa.* Rowland Ward, London.

* MATHEWS, G.M., 1928. *The Birds of Norfolk and Lord Howe Islands.* H.F. and G. Witherby Ltd, London.

* MATHEWS, G.M., 1933. On *Fregetta bonaparte* and allied genera. *Novitates Zoologicae 39,* 34–54.

MUGGLETON, J. and BENHAM, B.R., 1975. Isolation and decline of the large blue butterfly (*Macculinea arion*) in Great Britain. *Biological Conservation 7*, 119–128.

NIALL, I., 1980. *Portrait of a Country Artist. C.F. Tunnicliffe RA 1901–1979*. Victor Gollancz Ltd., London.

* OGILVIE-GRANT, W.R., 1911. On the Irish coal-titmouse (*Parus hibernicus*). *Ibis* 9th series, *5*, 548–552.

* OGILVIE-GRANT, W.R. and FORES, H.O., 1903. *The Natural History of Sokotra and Abdel-Kuri*. Porter, London.

RICHARDSON, E.W., 1916. *A Veteran Naturalist Being the Life and Work of W.B. Tegetmeier*. Witherby and Co., London.

RILEY, N.D., 1925. Review of *Natural History of British Butterflies*. *The Entomologist 58*, 43–45.

RILEY, N.D., 1947. F.W. Frohawk, *The Entomologist 80*, 25–27.

* ROTHSCHILD, L.W., 1893–1900. *The Avifauna of Laysan and the Neighbouring Islands*. R.H. Porter, London.

* ROTHSCHILD, W., 1894. Notes on *Sphingidae* with descriptions of new species. *Novitates Zoologicae 1*, 65–98.

* ROTHSCHILD, L.W., 1907. *Extinct Birds*. Hutchinson, London.

* ROTHSCHILD, L.W., 1909. *Nasua vittata* Tsch. *Novitates Zoologicae 16*, 333

* ROTHSCHILD, Lord, 1919. Algerian Lepidoptera. *Novitates Zoologicae 26*, 356–357.

* ROTHSCHILD, W., 1936. The genus *Dendrolagus*. *Transactions of the Zoological Society of London 21*, Part 6, 477–548.

* ROTHSCHILD, W. and HARTERT, E., 1899. A review of the ornithology of the Galapagos Islands with notes on the Webster-Harris Expedition. *Novitates Zoologicae 6*, 85–142.

ROTHSCHILD, M., 1983. *Dear Lord Rothschild. Birds, Butterflies and History*. Hutchinson, London.

ROTHSCHILD, M., 1985. A man of vision. *Natural World* No. 15, 54–56.

SCHERREN, H., n.d. *c.* 1905. *The Zoological Society of London*. Cassell and Co., London.

* SHUEL, R., 1938. Further notes on the eggs and nesting habits of birds in northern Nigeria (Kano Province). *Ibis* 14th series, *2*, 463–480.

SOUTH, R., 1896. The President's Address. *Proceedings of the South London Entomological and Natural History Society 1896*, 10–24.

STEARN, W., 1981. *The Natural History Museum at South Kensington*. Heinemann, London.

* TEGETMEIER, W.B., 1881. The rubiginous cat. *The Field 58*, 934.

TEGETMEIER, W.B., 1882. The sale of the African elephant. *The Field 59*, 250.

TEGETMEIER, W.B., 1883. Jumbo in America. *The Field 61*, 15.

* TEGETMEIER, W.B., 1883. The Moloch Monkey. *The Field 61*, 89.

* TEGETMEIER, W.B., 1884. The flying gecko at the Zoological Gardens. *The Field 64*, 487.

* TEGETMEIER, W.B., 1887. The zebras at the Zoological Gardens. *The Field 70*, 125.

* TEGETMEIER, W.B., 1888. Sale of an egg of the Great Auk. *The Field 71*, 387.

TEGETMEIER, W.B., 1889. The animals at Barnums. *The Field 74*, 709.

* TEGETMEIER, W.B., 1890. Breeding of Pallas's sand grouse in Scotland. *The Field 75*, 586.

* TEGETMEIER, W.B., 1893. Abnormal head of Kudu. *The Field 81*, 177.

* TEGETMEIER, W.B., 1893. The Goliath beetle at the Zoological Gardens. *The Field 82*, 607.

* TEGETMEIER, W.B., 1893. The young king vulture at the Zoological Gardens. *The Field 82*, 971.

TEGETMEIER, W.B., 1894. Bennett's tree kangaroos (*Dendrolagus bennetti*) in the Zoological Gardens, London. *The Field 84*, 991.

* TEGETMEIER, W.B., 1895. The South African giraffe at the Zoological Gardens. *The Field 85*, 310.

* TEGETMEIER, W.B., 1895. The three-banded armadillo (*Tolypeutes tricinctus*) in the Zoological Gardens. *The Field 85*, 633.

* TEGETMEIER, W.B., 1895. The frilled lizard at the Zoological Gardens. *The Field 86*, 218.

* TEGETMEIER, W.B., 1896. The gorilla at the Zoological Gardens. *The Field 87*, 481.

* TEGETMEIER, W.B., 1898. The siamang (*Hylobates syndactylus*). *The Field 92*, 858.

* TEGETMEIER, W.B., 1899. Grevy's zebra deposited by Her Majesty in the Zoological Gardens. *The Field 94*, 995.

* TEGETMEIER, W.B., 1901. *Okapia johnstoni*. *The Field 98*, 683.

* TEGETMEIER, W.B., 1911. *Pheasants for Coverts and Aviaries: Their Natural History and Practical Management* (5th edition). Horace Cox, London.

TEGETMEIER, W.B. and SUTHERLAND, C.L., 1895. *Horses, Asses, Zebras, Mules and Mule Breeding* (4th edition). Horace Cox, London.

TICEHURST, N.F., 1909. *A History of the Birds of Kent*. Witherby and Co., London.

TOMALIN, R., 1984. *W.H. Hudson – a Biography*. Oxford University Press.

TURNER, H.J., 1894. Notes on the fauna and flora of Wisley made during the Society's field meeting on July 7th. *Proceedings of the South London Entomological and Natural History Society 1894*, 87–90.

TUTT, J.W., 1899–1909. *A Natural History of the British Lepidoptera. A Text-book for Students and Collectors*. 10 volumes, Sonnenschein and Co., London and Friedlander and Son, Berlin.

VEVERS, G., 1976. *London's Zoo*. The Bodley Head, London.

* WALSH, J.H., 1886. *The Dogs of Britain, America and other Countries*. Field Office, London.

* WALSINGHAM, Rt. Hon. Lord, 1891. On the Micro-lepidoptera of the West Indies. *Proceedings of the Zoological Society of London 1891*, 492–549.

WALSINGHAM, Rt. Hon. Lord, 1907. Microlepidoptera of Tenerife. *Proceedings of the Zoological Society of London 1907*, 911–1034.

* WILSON, S.B., 1907. Notes on birds of Tahiti and the Society group. *Ibis, 1*, 373–379.

* WILSON, S.B. and EVANS, A.H., 1890–1899. *Aves Hawaiiensis: the Birds of the Sandwich Islands*. R.H. Porter, London.

YAXLEY, D., 1977. *Portrait of Norfolk*. Robert Hale, London.

ZUCKERMAN, Professor, Lord, 1976. *The Zoological Society of London 1826–1976 and Beyond*. Zoological Society of London and Academic Press.

Index